Gold EXPERIENCE

B2

First for Schools

Vocabulary and Grammar Workbook

T0345695

Mary Stephens

Contents

VOCABULARY

1 Find ten personality adjectives. The words go across, down or diagonally. The first letter of each word is highlighted.

m	i	t	a	s	p	a	y	n	e	l	l	o	r	t
z	p	b	e	o	q	r	x	s	p	o	i	l	e	d
p	n	l	j	c	o	c	a	r	i	n	g	k	k	n
n	n	m	o	i	m	o	v	x	l	o	o	n	p	h
n	o	i	t	a	d	u	a	m	z	w	u	x	t	q
c	o	t	p	b	p	j	n	g	x	u	t	s	b	q
g	e	g	i	l	x	r	v	e	v	m	s	h	o	d
h	y	t	u	e	o	q	v	l	x	o	p	y	s	q
o	p	g	a	b	d	r	j	e	r	o	o	a	s	j
m	h	f	b	h	e	u	i	b	f	d	k	y	y	o
a	j	u	d	w	e	g	o	r	u	y	e	w	z	b
s	t	l	l	v	n	c	t	i	s	r	n	v	l	l
s	h	t	h	x	c	o	w	t	s	e	z	k	g	p
v	v	o	e	x	f	o	o	y	y	f	w	f	d	u
p	k	l	p	n	l	l	u	n	c	e	b	i	o	g

2 Put the word in brackets in the correct place in the sentence.

1 We all wanted to win the race, but we couldn't keep _____*up*_____ with the leader. (up)
2 Skateboarding didn't use to be my thing, but I'm really it now! (into)
3 Nothing will ever put me dancing; I love it too much. (off)
4 I don't like drama lessons, so I'm planning to give them next term. (up)
5 You'll never stop Sonya from watching TV; she's completely addicted it. (to)
6 If I were better the guitar, I could join my friend's band. (at)

3 Put the words in order to make correct sentences.

1 was / plain / a / boring / He / a / black / wearing / tracksuit / .
   He was wearing a boring plain black tracksuit.
2 a / dress / dressed / in / flowery / knee-length / pink / She / was / .
   _____
3 baggy / relaxed / grey / in / comfortable / He / pants / .
   _____
4 dress / wore / She / short / a / stunning / woollen / .
   _____
5 in / amazing / a / blue / was / She / T-shirt / really / dressed / .
   _____
6 a / cotton / He / hoodie / navy / trendy / was / wearing / .
   _____
7 a / actress / beautiful / dress / silk / The / white / wore / .
   _____
8 blue / I / jeans / like / tight / wearing / denim / .

4 Complete the sentences with an appropriate word.

1 I'm sorry! I didn't mean to _____*hurt*_____ your feelings.
2 Zara has become a celebrity, but I'm sure she'll keep her _____ on the ground.
3 Relax - don't _____ life so seriously!
4 At weekends, I enjoy hanging _____ with my friends.
5 To get noticed, you need to _____ out from the crowd.
6 Failing the audition really knocked his _____ .
7 I'm very independent, so I like doing my _____ thing.
8 That singer's so famous he's become a household _____ .
9 I don't like classical ballet much, but I'm really _____ hip-hop.
10 Tom worries about everything, but his brother is much more laid- _____ .

5 Choose the correct answer, A, B or C.

1   Clare and I are _____ mates; we always go everywhere together.
    A top   (B) best   C first

2   My brother loves rock bands and I hate them, so we're total _____ when it comes to music.
    A opposites   B differences   C contrasts

3   Some brothers and sisters fight because of sibling _____ .
    A disagreement   B enmity   C rivalry

4   My penfriend and I are a perfect match because we have _____ interests.
    A same   B common   C equal

5   Sometimes I could murder my sister, other times I adore her; we have a real love-hate _____ .
    A relationship   B friendship   C partnership

6   Since Laura stole her friend's boyfriend they've been _____ enemies.
    A born   B torn   C sworn

7   Jason is one of my _____ friends and I'd trust him with my life!
    A nearest   B closest   C hardest

6 Complete the text with the best answer, A, B, C or D.

Who needs friends?

We all need friends to hang 1) _____ with. A really good friend is someone 2) _____ can share your secrets with and who is on your side when life gets tough. Most best mates have 3) _____ interests; they think the same and enjoy the same things you 4) _____ .
Of course, friendships between 5) _____ opposites are possible too, but these are less common. Remember that friends can disagree and even your 6) _____ friend may drive you crazy from time to time. If you're really unlucky, a friend can end up being your sworn 7) _____ , especially if they 'steal' your boyfriend or girlfriend! Even if you have a loyal best friend it's important that you keep 8) _____ new friends – if you always hang out with just one person, you'll forget how to socialise with other people and you'll end up being extremely boring yourself!

1   A up   B in   C out   D down
2   A they   B who   C that   D you
3   A equal   B common   C decided   D same
4   A are   B have   C do   D too
5   A complete   B decided   C whole   D great
6   A oldest   B grandest   C finest   D largest
7   A rivalry   B opposite   C competitor   D enemy
8   A forming   B making   C doing   D having

7 Complete the sentences with the correct form of the word in capitals.

1   I'm no longer on _speaking_ terms with my mum!   SPEAK

2   Clare is very _____ so I imagine she'll end up as an artist or a sculptor.   CREATE

3   That boy changes his girlfriend every week – he's got no idea of _____ at all!   LOYAL

4   Thanks to my grandad's _____ , I've got enough money to buy a car!   GENEROUS

5   Sandra isn't very pretty, but her sister's extremely _____ .   BEAUTY

6   Being _____ and ordering people about is never going to make you popular!   BOSS

7   There's a lot of _____ between my sister and I.   RIVAL

8   Have you got a good _____ with your parents?   RELATION

9   She and her ex-boyfriend are _____ enemies!   SWEAR

10   One day, I would like to be rich and _____ .   SUCCEED

8 Complete the words in the sentences.

1   My sister is very ungrateful; she takes everything for gr _a_ _n_ _t_ _ ed.

2   Laura stole Emma's boyfriend, which destroyed their r _____ a _____ p.

3   Tom's completely ob _____ d with dancing; he thinks of nothing else.

4   George is a tr _____ tt _____ ; all his friends try to copy his clothes and his behaviour.

5   My friend is a complete r _____ and opposes everyone in authority!

6   My brother goes to lots of auditions, but all he gets are r _ j _____ on _____ .

7   She's always so s _____ b _____ n! She refuses to change her mind no matter how you try to persuade her.

8   My little brother is completely s _____ d; my parents give him everything he wants.

GRAMMAR
Grammar focus: present and present perfect tenses

1 Complete the table and then complete the sentences below.

	Infinitive	Past simple	Past participle
1	buy	bought	*bought*
2	fall	fell	
3	know	knew	
4	meet	met	
5	sing	sang	
6	steal	stole	

a My parents *have bought* me a brilliant computer game for my birthday!

b Oh no! Someone _____ my MP3 player!

c _____ you _____ Robert's new girlfriend yet?

d I _____ out with my neighbour. We never speak to each other nowadays.

e My brother _____ with some of the most famous bands in our country; he's playing in our town next week.

f I _____ Emma for long, but she's definitely my best friend now.

2 Put the words in the correct order.

1 instead of studying / playing / always / My brother / computer games / is / .
   My brother is always playing computer games instead of studying.

2 seen / that clip / I / have / on / before / YouTube / never / .

3 wanted / to be / She / always / an actress / has / .

4 living / for ten years / have / here / been / We / .

5 have / How long / drama / studying / you / been?

6 arranged / in the park / We / just / have / to meet / .

7 yet / that dance / learnt / you / Have?

8 has been / March / a video / Our class / since / making / .

3 Choose the correct answer, A, B or C.

1 I can't come out because I _____ my homework.
   A am doing
   B do
   C have done

2 My brother annoys me because he _____.
   A is never listening
   B never listens
   C never is listening

3 How many texts _____ so far today?
   A have you sent
   B did you send
   C are you sending

4 I _____ to be famous.
   A have never been wanting
   B am never wanting
   C have never wanted

5 I'm sweating because I _____.
   A have jogged
   B am being jogging
   C have been jogging

6 Can you play the guitar well? No, I _____ to learn it.
   A have just started
   B have just been starting
   C just have started

7 Sorry I'm late! How long _____?
   A are you waiting
   B have you been waiting
   C have you waited

8 _____ acting?
   A Have you always been loving
   B Are you always loving
   C Have you always loved

4 Choose the correct verb form.

1 *I've finished/I've been finishing/I finish* the book now so you can have it if you like.

2 How many slices of pizza *are you eating/have you eaten/have you been eating* so far?

3 She hasn't slept because *she's travelled/she travels/she's been travelling*.

4 Emma's really annoying – she *always is bossing/is always bossing/bosses always* my friends around.

5 How long *have you known/are you knowing/have you been knowing* your best friend?

6 When *I'm not studying/I haven't studied/I don't study,* I hang out with my friends.

Grammar focus: present perfect or past simple?

5 Put the verbs in brackets into the correct tense, present perfect or past simple.

1 We ____*formed*____ our rock band about a year ago. (form)

2 He's tired because he _____ a long way. (run).

3 I _____ anyone when I arrived at the party. (not/recognise)

4 I'm worried about Barry because he _____ me for ages. (not/text)

5 They _____ abroad for two years before moving here. (live)

6 When _____ school? (she/leave)

7 Why _____ Paul _____ anyone that he'd finished with his girlfriend? (not/tell)

8 Sarah _____ a great video from YouTube the other day. (download)

9 Oh no, I _____ my phone! (lose)

10 For my last birthday, my parents _____ for me to learn the guitar. (pay)

6 Rewrite the sentences so they have a similar meaning. Use the word in brackets.

1 How long have you been training to be an actor? (start)

   When did you start training to be an actor?

2 How long ago did you meet your best friend? (since)

   How long is it _____ your best friend?

3 I have been driving for six months. (began)

   I _____ .

4 My sister keeps annoying me all the time. (always)

   My sister _____ me.

5 How much experience do you have in playing tennis? (have)

   How long _____ tennis?

6 I've never seen a better singer than him. (ever)

   He's the best singer _____ .

7 The match only started a minute ago. (just)

   The match _____ .

8 Clare has never acted on TV before. (first)

   This is the _____ on TV.

7 Put the verbs in the correct tense.

Dogs 1) __*have been*__ (be) man's best friend from early times. We 2) _____ (always/read) about dogs that go missing and then take incredibly long journeys to find their owners. A few years ago, a stray dog in China 3) _____ (run) behind a group of cyclists for twenty-four hours. He 4) _____ (travel) over 1,500 kilometres! Happily, one of the cyclists finally 5) _____ (decide) to give him a home.

8 Use the clues to complete the crossword.

Across

2 A person who starts doing something that everybody else follows

3 An adjective for someone who seems relaxed and not worried about anything

5 _____ people enjoy meeting other people.

6 This is another word for *brothers and sisters*.

9 An adjective for someone who is very careful what they choose and is difficult to please

10 If you give _____ something, you stop doing it.

Down

1 People sometimes have a love-hate _____ .

4 The past participle of *wear*

7 Another adjective for *courageous*

8 Another adjective for *talented*

Revision Unit 1

1 Complete the sentences with an appropriate preposition.

1 Where do you hang _____out_____ most weekends?
2 Are you addicted _____ rap music or do you hate it?
3 Do you get on well _____ most of your classmates?
4 What kind of bad behaviour puts you _____ people?
5 Would you find it easy to give _____ using your mobile phone?
6 Are you the kind of person who stands _____ from the crowd?
7 My brother is obsessed _____ skateboarding.
8 It's expensive trying to keep _____ with the latest trends.

2 Choose the correct answer, A, B or C.

1 I have a lot in _____ with my sister.
   A line   B common   C use
2 Well done, but don't let success go to your _____.
   A head   B heart   C brain
3 If you're independent, you like _____ your own thing.
   A being   B saying   C doing
4 I wish Paul didn't always _____ life so seriously!
   A make   B do   C take
5 I'm sorry if I _____ your feelings.
   A hurt   B damaged   C knocked
6 Keep your feet on the _____ and don't let success spoil you.
   A path   B ground   C earth
7 Shy people sometimes don't want to stand out from the _____.
   A group   B friends   C crowd
8 Clive wants everyone to notice him; he's a terrible _____.
   A show-off   B bully   C rebel

3 Choose the correct answer.

1 He was wearing *baggy, long pants/long, baggy pants* and a T-shirt.
2 I like *cotton, trendy T-shirts/trendy, cotton T-shirts*.
3 She's got some *blue, beautiful, denim jeans/beautiful, blue, denim jeans*.
4 My sister's bought herself *a fantastic, loose, woollen sweater/a woollen, fantastic, loose sweater*.
5 Dad's got several *cream, linen, plain suits/plain, cream, linen suits*.
6 The model was wearing a *stunning, red, knee-length dress/knee-length, red, stunning dress*.
7 George looked good in his *silk purple/purple silk* shirt and tie.
8 Clare liked that *short, tight, leather skirt/tight, leather, short skirt*, but her mum wouldn't let her buy it.

4 Use the correct form of the word in capitals to fill each gap.

1 Don't be so _____fussy_____! FUSS
2 My parents love to _____ with friends in their free time. SOCIAL
3 You don't need to be so _____ about everything! SARCASM
4 My dad's jokes are actually quite _____. FUN
5 Doctors need to be very kind and _____ people. CARE
6 Fiona's a very _____ sort of girl, so she won't get into any trouble. SENSE
7 My mum's so unselfish and _____! THINK
8 Stop behaving like a _____ child! SPOIL

5 Complete the collocations by matching the words.

1 sibling   a interests
2 love-hate   b trends
3 total   c mates
4 a household   d rivalry
5 sworn   e relationship
6 the latest   f opposites
7 common   g name
8 best   h enemies

6 Put the words in the correct order.

1 he / hours / is / It / left / since / three / .
It is three hours since he left.

2 a / band / been / for / Has / in / long / she / the / time / ?
_____

3 always / asking / bossy / girl / is / questions / that / Why / ?
_____

4 Did / hear / I / just / said / what / you / ?
_____

5 penfriend / Have / to / written / yet / you / your / ?
_____

6 best / ever / film / have / I / is / seen / That / the / .
_____

7 ages / did / discover / for / not / secret / the / We / .
_____

8 a / am / getting / I / job / next / of / temporary / thinking / year / .
_____

7 Complete the spaces in the text with an appropriate word.

8 Rewrite the sentences using the words in capitals.

1 He began painting some years ago.   FOR
He has been painting ___*for a year*___ .

2 My friends have a habit of teasing me.   ARE
My friends _____ me.

3 This is his first experience of appearing on TV.   NEVER
He _____ on TV before.

4 It's ages since I've been to this park.   NOT
I _____ this park for ages.

5 The band haven't played together for a month.   SINCE
It's a month _____ together.

6 This watch is not mine.   BELONG
This watch _____ me.

7 I haven't been to the cinema since July.   TIME
The last _____ the cinema was July.

8 They've been here for ten minutes.   AGO
They _____ .

9 I'm still reading.   NOT
I _____ yet.

10 I need a reliable friend.   ON
I need a friend I can _____ .

Girlfriend problems?

Calling all you guys out there! 1) ___*Have*___ you ever had problems choosing the right girlfriend? Are you good 2) _____ forming new relationships, or 3) _____ you sometimes get things quite wrong? Before you give 4) _____ on relationships completely, let me give you some advice. Many of you guys 5) _____ competitive and like showing off to your mates, right? Hanging 6) _____ with a beautiful girlfriend may seem like the ideal way to do this. Perhaps you think it makes you stand 7) _____ from the crowd? Well, it's not a clever idea at all! Just 8) _____ a girl looks good, it doesn't mean she has a personality. She may end up boring you to death! No, date a girl with a beautiful mind and then your friends will really envy you.

02 Wild

VOCABULARY

1 Complete the words in the sentences.

1 Diana doesn't fit in. She's such a teacher's p_e_t!
2 Animals like lions and wolves p_____y on other animals.
3 Most dogs are happy if you st_____ them.
4 Fishermen often sl_____er sharks in their thousands.
5 You can't stop yourself when you need to sneeze – it's a re_____x action.
6 Hedgehogs roll up in a ball when they're in danger – it's a def_____e mechanism.
7 I didn't use to like birdwatching, but now I'm h_____ed – I do it all the time!
8 A fish needs f_____s in order to swim properly.

2 Identify the animals in the pictures and complete the sentences below.

 A

 B

 C

 D

 E

 F

 G

1 _F_ A _gorilla_ is a great ape that can walk on two legs.
2 ___ A_____ can be extremely venomous.
3 ___ A_____ lives in the ocean and preys on other fish.
4 ___ A_____ has striped skin and striped fur.
5 ___ A_____ swallows stones and can regrow all its sharp teeth.
6 ___ A_____ hunts seals on the sea ice.
7 ___ A_____ has a hard shell and eats jellyfish.

3 Choose the correct answer, A, B, C or D.

1 To save endangered animals, we need to protect their _____ from destruction.
   A areas   B regions
   C homes   **D** habitats
2 The emission of _____ gases may be altering the climate of our planet.
   A greenhouse   B global
   C solar   D warming
3 Tigers are an endangered _____.
   A sort   B type
   C category   D species
4 Some dry places are becoming deserts because of _____ erosion.
   A land   B soil
   C ground   D earth
5 When there's a heat _____, there's a risk of forest fires.
   A stroke   B storm
   C wave   D rise
6 When we burn fossil _____, we pollute the atmosphere.
   A fires   B oils
   C caps   D fuels
7 Large parts of the rainforest are disappearing due to illegal _____.
   A cutting   B chopping
   C logging   D sticking
8 Our weather may get more extreme because of climate _____.
   A alteration   B change
   C movement   D wave

4 Choose the correct phrasal verb.

1 They've *set up/set by/set on* a new company in town selling solar panels.
2 If you *run up/run out of/run through* pet food, your dog won't be too happy!
3 My dad *gave out/gave off/gave up* driving last year – he goes everywhere by bike now.
4 That tree is dying; they'll need to *cut it up/ cut it down/cut it off* soon.
5 Companies should make products that can be repaired, not just *thrown down/thrown away/thrown up*.
6 The music is too loud in here! Can you *turn it up/turn it in/turn it down*, please?

5 Write the opposite meaning of these adjectives in the correct box below.

> ~~logical~~ experienced formal happy honest legal obedient polite possible practical relevant responsible reversible satisfied x2

Il-	Ir-	Im-
illogical		

In-	Dis-	Un-

6 Complete the sentences with the correct form of the word in capitals.

1 I'm *unhappy* about the numbers of animals that are endangered. **HAPPY**

2 People who drop rubbish in the street are so _____! **RESPONSIBLE**

3 Driving above the speed limit is not just _____, it is bad for the environment, too. **LEGAL**

4 Those plans won't work because they are too _____. **PRACTICAL**

5 If global temperatures rise by more than 2%, the effects on the planet might be _____. **REVERSIBLE**

6 The zookeeper who was attacked by the tiger was young and _____. **EXPERIENCED**

7 My puppy is really _____, so I'm taking him for proper training classes. **OBEDIENT**

8 Companies that lie about the amount of energy they use are being _____. **HONEST**

7 Use the clues to complete the crossword.

Across

1 A violent crash involving two or more cars

5 A word that means *not bothered*

8 If you don't have an alarm clock, you may do this.

9 Jeans and T-shirts are an _____ way to dress.

Down

2 An _____ is someone who owns or runs a factory or company.

3 Another word for *rude*

4 If something is _____, you pay too much for it.

6 You need a lot of imagination and _____ to be a great artist.

7 Something like a box or bowl that you keep things in

8 Complete the text with the correct form of the words in capitals.

Designing for nature

For decades 1) *scientists* have warned us that global 2) _____ is a major threat to our planet. There is a danger that our planet will overheat and that the resulting natural disasters may 3) _____ life on earth. The materials designers and technologists use to manufacture products must be chosen carefully. Most metals are easy to 4) _____, so these are fine to use. The plastic used in some kinds of plastic 5) _____ can be reused as well, but oil-based plastic is not biodegradable, so anything made with this material can be a major cause of 6) _____.

SCIENCE
WARM

DANGER

CYCLE

CONT AIN

POLLUTE

GRAMMAR
Grammar focus: past tenses

1 Choose the correct verb form.

1 I *was walking/walked/had been walking* for ten minutes when I came across the injured fox.
2 We sheltered in our tent because it *rained/it was raining/it had rained*.
3 My neighbour used to have a pet snake, but it *was always escaping/had always been escaping/had always escaped*, so he got rid of it.
4 The bull *saw/was seeing* the dog, *chased/was chasing* it across the field and *was then throwing/then threw/had then thrown* it up in the air.
5 The cheetah was exhausted because it *was running/had been running/ran* at top speed for quite some time.
6 The park was in complete darkness because the sun *had gone/went/was going* down.
7 I bet you *were feeling scared/felt scared/had felt scared* when the lion appeared in front of you!
8 *Did the tiger kill/Had the tiger killed/Had the tiger been killing* the cub by the time the ranger arrived?

2 Complete the sentences with the correct form of the verb in brackets.

1 When we got back from the safari, a TV company _was waiting_ to interview us. (wait)
2 Because it .... all day, we were able to see the bear's tracks very clearly. (snow)
3 While I .... on a rock, I spotted a shark circling out at sea. (sit)
4 Zoologists trekked through the mountains for days because they .... to find a snow leopard. (want)
5 The whale was the most amazing animal we ....! (ever see)
6 After a week in the jungle, the cameramen .... millions of photos. (already/take)
7 The minute we .... that the elephant was in trouble, we ran to get help. (realise)
8 It was ages since I .... a horse. (last/ride)
9 How long .... the deer before the lions arrived? (you/watch)
10 We were excited because we .... on a wildlife holiday before. (never/go)

3 Use the prompts to make correct sentences.

1 How long / you / dive / before / you / see / the turtle?
   How long had you been diving before you saw the turtle?
2 As we watched, the zebra / lift / its head and / look / at us.
3 They could see that the cat / already eat / the mouse / because / there / be only bones left.
4 While / the biologists / explore / the cave, / they / discover / a rare species of bat.
5 she / scream / very loudly / when / she / see / the scorpion?
6 Volunteers / rescue / the injured seal and / keep / it in a sanctuary until it / be / healthy again.
7 By the time she / get / her camera out, / the leopard / disappear.
8 The wolves / follow / the buffalo / for an hour / before the snowstorm / arrive.

4 Complete the article with one word in each space.

DANGER IN THE DARK!

Animals 1) _have_ escaped from captivity many times over the years. However, a few years 2) .... there was a mass escape of wild animals. The state police described it as the worst event they 3) .... ever encountered. They had all 4) .... hoping for a quiet night when the first calls came into the office. Callers reported seeing bears, big cats, and other dangerous beasts which 5) .... running loose along the highway! At first the police 6) .... not know whether to believe the stories, but when they visited the wild animals preserve they saw the fence 7) .... broken and the cages were empty. It took a long time to round up the animals – big cats were hiding up trees in the dark so the situation was extremely dangerous! People had to to stay indoors and schools were closed 8) .... several days. A free holiday then, but what a scary reason to get off class!

Grammar focus: used to, get used to, would

5 Complete the sentences by matching the parts.

1 As a small child, I always	a used to living in the country.
2 Did you	b getting used to working in a zoo?
3 Will you ever	c use to keep chickens?
4 Tanya can't get	d get used to eating insects!
5 Years ago, I would	e to work as a wildlife cameraman.
6 Adam used	f get used to sleeping on the ground?
7 We'll never	g never go near a spider.
8 Are you	h used to help my mum feed the chickens.

6 Choose the correct answer, A, B or C.

1 We're not used _____ horses.
 A to ride
 B riding
 C to riding ✓

2 Did you know that my grandad _____ a vet?
 A would be
 B used to be
 C use to be

3 When we lived on a farm, we _____ help Dad milk the cows.
 A would always
 B always would
 C use always to

4 As a child, _____ scared of dogs?
 A would you be
 B did you use to be
 C use you to be

5 Our pet rabbit _____ spoiled by all of us.
 A always used to be
 B was always used to be
 C always would be

6 The boys _____ working with animals.
 A aren't used to
 B don't use to
 C used not to

7 When my sister was a baby, she _____ elephants laid eggs!
 A would think
 B used to thinking
 C used to think

7 Complete the text with one word in each space.

When we were younger, our parents used to take us into the countryside 1) ___*at*___ the weekend. We 2) _____ walk a few kilometres and then sit down to picnic. Once, we stopped to eat in a large field. We 3) _____ only just unpacked our picnic when we heard a deafening roar. We looked round quickly - and saw a huge bull watching us! This bull was clearly not 4) _____ to humans. It had 5) _____ sleeping peacefully and 6) _____ not appreciate being woken up. From the way it moved its head, we could see it 7) _____ planning to charge. 8) _____ the time we'd jumped to our feet, the bull was nearly upon us. What on earth were we going to do?

8 Complete the verbs in each sentence.

1 I was scared so my heart was b e a t i n g very fast.

2 We were wearing wet suits because we'd been d_____g.

3 My brother picked up the snake although I b_____g_____ him not to.

4 Sandra's hamster had got out of its cage and d_____r_____d.

5 The hunters sl_____t_____r_____d hundreds of sharks.

6 While we were sitting in the forest, a deer suddenly c_____s_____ through the trees near us.

7 Our teacher o_____i_____ for us to go on a wildlife trip.

8 We listened carefully until we_____a_____d the sound of horses' hooves.

Revision Unit 2

1 Complete the table with the missing word forms.

	Verb	Adjective	Noun
1	emit	xxxxxx	emission
2	conserve	conservative	
3	xxxxxx		environment
4	erode	eroded	
5		threatening	threat
6		dangerous/	danger
7	pollute		
8		industrial	(person)

2 Complete the sentences with the correct form of the word in capitals.

1 Cutting down forests can cause soil _____erosion_____ . ERODE

2 Dad has _____ to sell my dog if it doesn't stop barking all night! THREAT

3 Fumes from cars and lorries cause a great deal of _____ . POLLUTE

4 _____ organisations work to highlight the dangers posed by greenhouse gases. ENVIRONMENT

5 As more countries _____ , the need to protect our planet grows more urgent. INDUSTRY

6 Many zoos regard _____ as one of their major roles. CONSERVE

7 Polar bears are increasingly seen as an _____ species because the ice they hunt on is melting. DANGER

8 Industries guilty of the _____ of greenhouse gases may be fined a lot of money. EMIT

9 Illegal _____ is destroying large sections of this planet's rainforests. LOG

10 Some industries still use too much packaging, such as unnecessary plastic food _____ . CONTAIN

3 Complete the collocations by adding one word.

1 If we want to be 'green', instead of driving cars we should use _____public_____ transport.

2 A long period of extremely hot weather is called a heat _____ .

3 _____ fuels like coal and oil are formed from the remains of prehistoric plants and animals.

4 Our seas are getting warmer due to climate _____ .

5 Some weather forecasters say global _____ will give Europe wet, cold summers for many years.

6 _____ power is the result of converting sunlight into electricity.

7 Sea levels are rising because the Arctic _____ caps are melting.

8 _____ gases like carbon dioxide increase the temperature of our planet.

4 Complete the sentences with an appropriate preposition.

1 Madison set _____up_____ her own film company.

2 They've cut _____ our beautiful palm trees to make way for a car park.

3 It's quite warm today so you can turn _____ the heating a bit.

4 One day we may run _____ of fossil fuels.

5 Don't forget to switch _____ the lights if you're the last to leave.

6 Why not give your old clothes to charity shops instead of throwing them _____ ?

7 I'm going to give _____ eating meat and become a vegetarian.

8 We must go _____ fighting to conserve nature and never give up.

5 Choose the correct answer, A, B or C.

1 They were the scariest animals we _____ .
  A ever saw
  B were ever seeing
  C had ever seen

2 The zoo _____ have so many animals as it has now.
  A didn't use to
  B wouldn't
  C used to not

3 By the time I got home, the sun _____ down.
  A had already been going
  B had already gone
  C already was going

4 The company was fined because they _____ chemicals in the river for months.
  A had dumped
  B were dumping
  C had been dumping

5 We nearly killed the frogs because we _____ caring for amphibians.
  A weren't used to
  B didn't use to
  C used not to

6 While you _____ this morning, I was out birdwatching.
  A had still slept
  B were still sleeping
  C had still been sleeping

6 Complete the article with one word in each space.

Bob the street cat

James Bowen used 1) _to_ be a lonely busker. Every day he 2) _____ sit in the street and play his battered old guitar to earn money. He was 3) _____ to being alone. But that all changed 4) _____ Bob the cat arrived at his flat. James didn't really want a pet, but as Bob had been sitting on his doorstep 5) _____ three days, he invited him in. Bob was badly injured – a fox or another cat 6) _____ attacked him - so James nursed him back to health. After that, Bob followed him everywhere, even on the bus! Soon they 7) _____ even busking together and Bob became a star on YouTube!

7 Complete the second sentence so it has a similar meaning to the first, using the word in capitals. Do not use more than five words.

1 On my arrival, I started exploring my surroundings.
  AS
  I started exploring my surroundings _as soon as I arrived_ .

2 It was his first experience of seeing tigers. BEFORE
  He _____ .

3 Their journey took three days so they were very tired.
  FOR
  They were very tired because they _____ _____ three days.

4 During the filming, the cameramen got stung by bees.
  WHILE
  The cameramen got stung by bees _____ _____ .

5 They haven't seen the gorilla for two days. LAST
  It's two days _____ a gorilla.

6 The weather changed before my departure. LEFT
  By _____ , the weather had changed.

7 The bull charged before the walkers had finished eating their picnic.
  STILL
  The bull charged while the walkers _____ _____ picnic.

8 It was the best experience of her life. EVER
  It was the best experience she _____ _____ .

8 Find ten words on the topic of the environment. The words go across, down or diagonally. The first letter of each word is highlighted.

b	i	m	e	l	g	h	a	n	d	k	n	j	f	c
w	w	i	l	d	l	i	f	e	u	o	x	m	k	e
c	c	l	i	m	a	t	e	a	i	z	z	j	o	r
s	p	j	y	w	n	m	p	t	v	g	n	w	g	o
n	o	k	h	e	n	d	a	n	g	e	r	e	d	s
q	l	u	n	z	a	v	m	n	l	b	y	l	b	i
y	l	h	l	l	r	s	w	k	v	q	d	o	k	o
n	u	f	d	e	o	p	h	p	e	i	y	g	s	n
s	t	o	s	u	f	e	a	i	c	l	o	g	c	l
p	i	n	k	l	r	c	b	g	o	s	q	i	o	k
l	o	p	c	i	d	i	i	f	l	h	b	n	r	g
c	n	e	p	p	e	e	t	u	o	y	t	g	l	u
i	w	m	b	q	s	s	a	v	g	k	q	r	p	q
g	u	h	l	q	h	n	t	a	y	b	j	p	i	q

Awesome science

VOCABULARY

1 Complete the sentences with these words.

> aliens   doomed   gravity   ~~planet~~
> predictions   robot   satellite   weird

1 The Earth is not a star; it is a ___planet___ .
2 The very first _____, called Sputnik, was launched into space back in 1957.
3 From time to time, people claim they have seen _____ arrive on Earth in flying saucers!
4 Without the force of _____ we would all float off into space.
5 I find the idea of parallel universes really _____ .
6 Don't you wish they'd build a _____ that would do your homework for you?
7 If you ever fell into a black hole, you could never escape – you'd be _____ !
8 Physicists can't prove all their theories, but they have made some amazing _____ about the nature of the universe.

2 Match a word from the box with each of the lists below.

> astronomy   chemistry   geology
> mathematics   ~~physics~~   technology

1 ___physics___
  black holes
  parallel universe

2 _____
  numbers
  patterns
  shapes
  problems
  logical

3 _____
  machines
  gadgets
  equipment
  kits

4 _____
  solar eclipse
  planets
  stars
  space
  galaxy

5 _____
  test tubes
  experiments
  acids
  gases
  substances

6 _____
  rock formations
  fossils
  dinosaur bone

3 Choose the correct word, A, B, C or D.

1 My chemistry teacher says I'm _____ a lot of progress.
  A doing   B having
  C getting   (D) making
2 The technician hasn't managed to _____ the air conditioning yet.
  A heal   B cure
  C fix   D solve
3 I wish I'd _____ more attention in class!
  A done   B paid
  C made   D lent
4 Have you written up the experiment we _____ in class yesterday?
  A did   B got
  C made   D used
5 Turn down the heating to _____ energy.
  A preserve   B save
  C spare   D limit
6 Can somebody tell me how to _____ this machine?
  A control   B run
  C perform   D work
7 Our new chemistry teacher got the job because she _____ lots of previous experience.
  A got   B owned
  C did   D had
8 Some chemicals have _____ missing from the laboratory!
  A gone   B ended
  C resulted   D come

4 Choose the correct preposition.

1 The teacher told us to get *up/in/on* with our work.
2 My experiment turned *up/in/out* better than I thought it would.
3 They're going to shut *off/down/out* our local chemical factory.
4 The chemist's attempts to heat the substance ended *up/out/of* as a disaster.
5 Can you take *round/on/over* this task from me while I answer the phone?
6 We're not allowed to copy; we've got to come *up/in/over* with our own ideas!

5 Complete the sentences by matching the parts.

1. A test tube is a finger-shaped and U-shaped glass object
2. A thermometer is a glass device
3. Scales are instruments
4. A beaker is a cylindrical container with a flat bottom
5. A telescope is an instrument
6. A calculator is a device

a. used to measure the weight of things.
b. used to perform sums and calculations.
c. used to help you view faraway objects, like stars.
d. used to hold small quantities of chemicals.
e. used to measure temperature.
f. used to stir, mix, and heat liquids in.

6 Complete the sentences with a correct preposition.

1. Recently, there's been an increase _____in_____ the temperature on our planet.
2. Our teacher insists _____ accuracy.
3. Who is responsible _____ breaking the test tube?
4. My sister has a real talent _____ physics.
5. I think I'd benefit _____ a long holiday!
6. Can I rely _____ Paul or not?
7. We were ashamed _____ our chemistry test results.
8. There was no lack _____ interest when our teacher suggested a trip to the Science Museum.

7 Complete the article with the correct form of the words in capitals.

8 Find ten words on the topic of science. The words go across, down or diagonally. The first letter of each word has been highlighted for you.

u	t	s	b	k	r	t	e	l	e	s	c	o	p	e
u	s	k	g	d	f	s	a	t	e	l	l	i	t	e
n	d	e	n	n	w	y	l	w	q	h	h	f	e	o
i	i	x	l	p	t	i	a	i	f	x	b	r	n	d
v	v	p	f	w	h	f	b	r	e	l	q	t	t	b
e	f	e	z	d	e	r	o	u	i	f	n	e	c	g
r	g	r	x	r	e	x	r	e	q	e	n	d	h	l
s	s	i	e	k	o	p	a	t	m	a	k	e	n	e
e	e	m	a	b	i	b	t	n	l	p	k	e	q	y
m	t	e	v	c	g	i	o	p	n	z	i	j	t	v
c	b	n	d	a	h	r	r	t	t	l	r	f	j	e
s	l	t	e	l	i	i	y	k	a	z	n	p	l	l
t	f	g	f	v	f	h	u	v	r	q	i	u	s	s
l	d	u	n	k	s	z	a	r	t	i	s	t	l	x
u	g	e	k	t	g	r	a	v	i	t	y	z	u	h

Life on Mars?

Year by year, our little planet is becoming 1) _overcrowded_ As the human population continues to grow, 2) _____ are looking for planets which humans could colonise. One popular 3) _____ is that Mars will be our new home. However, it is icy cold and has very little carbon dioxide. At present, humans would be 4) _____ to survive there. But the big difference in the atmospheric 5) _____ of Earth and Mars hasn't stopped people from dreaming! One 6) _____ experts have made for heating up the planet is to build 'greenhouse gas factories'. They say these factories could take in carbon dioxide and give out oxygen, just as plants do on Earth. As 7) _____ as it may seem, these ideas may become reality one day. However, humans are 8) _____ to be living on Mars for many centuries to come.

CROWDED
SCIENCE
PREDICT

ABLE
CHEMIST
SUGGEST

CREDIBLE
LIKELY

GRAMMAR
Grammar focus: the future

1 Choose the correct answer, A, B or C.

1 While you're having your interview tomorrow, I _____ my grandparents.
   A am visiting (B) will be visiting C visit

2 As soon as I _____ my new telescope, I'll take a course in astronomy.
   A will get B am getting C get

3 At some point in the future, scientists _____ send a manned spacecraft to Mars.
   A are going to B go to C will be going to

4 We're going to test the liquid after it _____ .
   A is cooling B will cool C cools

5 What _____ this evening? Would you like to come out with me?
   A will you do B are you doing C do you do?

6 While my dad _____ the lecture, I'll be sitting in the audience!
   A is giving B will be giving C will have given

2 Complete the mini dialogues with the appropriate form of the verb in brackets.

1 A: Don't worry. I'll switch out the lights when I _____go_____ (go).
   B: Thanks!

2 A: _____ (you/not go) to the Science Fair this afternoon? You'll be sorry if you miss it!
   B: Don't worry, I put my name down ages ago!

3 A: What time are they expecting you at the planetarium?
   B: The performance _____ (start) at 9 a.m. sharp – I've checked on the programme. We'll get there some time before that.

4 A: We _____ (sit) in a biology lesson this time tomorrow – as usual! What about you?
   B: Oh, we've got a holiday day tomorrow. Hurray!

5 A: By the time it comes back to earth next week, that satellite _____ (travel) round the Earth for six months.
   B: Wow, that's incredible!

6 A: I _____ (study) science at university. That's my plan, anyway.
   B: Well good luck. I hope you do well at it!

3 Use the prompts to make correct future sentences.

1 I / go / cinema tonight
   I am going to the cinema tonight.

2 By this time next year / we / move house.

3 At 10 a.m. tomorrow you'll be at home, but I / fly / over the Pacific!

4 I / send / you a text as soon as I / hear / the news.

5 The teacher says he / buy / some new test tubes / when / he / get / the chance.

6 Hurry up! The chemistry lesson / start / in five minutes!

7 After we / finish / learning about frogs, / we / go on / to another bit of the biology syllabus.

8 My sister Tanya / leave / school / by the time / I / be / in my final year.

4 Complete the sentences with the correct word.

1 It's possible that the teacher won't give us homework, but it isn't _____likely_____!

2 We're _____ to get in to the gig because we don't have tickets.

3 Do you know what time the plane is due _____ land?

4 We _____ going to take the bus, but Sally has decided to walk instead.

5 It's very _____ to snow, so don't go walking in the mountains.

6 Hurry up! The lecture _____ about to start.

Grammar focus: future in the past

5 **Choose the correct answer, A or B.**

1 I'm not about to handle that snake!
  A I'm not going to do it.
  B I don't know how to do it.

2 You're likely to fail if you don't try harder.
  A It's probable you'll fail.
  B There's a small chance you'll fail.

3 I'm not due to see the headmaster until 4 p.m.
  A I have no intention of seeing him.
  B He's not expecting me until then.

4 I wasn't going to apologise to Sarah, but there we are!
  A I apologised.
  B I didn't apologise.

5 The train was due to leave at 11 a.m..
  A According to my opinion
  B According to the timetable

6 It's unlikely to rain.
  A It probably won't rain.
  B People don't want it to rain.

7 The movie is about to start.
  A It's going to start at any minute.
  B It's already started.

8 They were going to train as astronauts.
  A They did their training.
  B They didn't do their training.

6 **Choose the correct answer, A, B or C.**

1 The project might be ready on time, but it's _____ .
  A unsure   **B** impossible   **C** unlikely

2 The rain started as the tennis match was _____ to begin.
  A likely   **B** around   **C** about

3 They _____ going to launch the rocket today, but it's been cancelled.
  A were   **B** are   **C** weren't

4 I'm just _____ to get on the train, so I'll have to text you when I've found a seat.
  A about   **B** due   **C** likely

5 I thought you were _____ to meet me last night as planned. What happened?
  A due   **B** going   **C** about

6 I'm very sorry, but my essay is _____ to be finished on time.
  A impossible   **B** unsure   **C** unlikely

7 **Complete the text with one appropriate word in each space. Use any word *once* only.**

www.newfirst.com

Scientists have recently come up with 1) ___*an*___ amazing invention. Imagine the scene. You 2) _____ about to rob a bank – but then a policeman comes and stands right next to you. You're unlikely 3) _____ try and rob the bank now, correct? But the invention I'm 4) _____ to describe might make robbery a lot easier in the future! I actually saw this wonderful bit of technology at a special video demonstration. The demonstration was 5) _____ to take place at 09.00 prompt, so I got to the university 6) _____ good time. At the start of the demonstration, a cat climbed into a tank. That's not very exciting, we thought. What we didn't realise was that the cat 7) _____ about to vanish in front of our eyes, by means of an 'invisibility cloak'! This new device hides objects by bending light in different directions. Sadly for robbers, however, it 8) _____ unlikely to be in the shops any time soon!

8 **Correct the word in italics in each of these sentences.**

1 The exam results are due *for* be published today!
  The exam results are due to be published today.

2 You're *likely* to see a lot of stars if it's cloudy tonight.

3 Mum's *about* to go on a lecture tour next month.

4 We *are* going to take our holiday in June, but we've had to change the date to July.

5 Paul wasn't *due* to ask Sonya out, but he couldn't stop himself.

6 Sh! The lecture is just *ready* to start.

7 According to the timetable, our plane is *likely* to take off in ten minutes' time.

8 Look out! That car was just *due* to run you over!

Revision Unit 3

1 Complete the sentences.

1 A person who studies numbers and shapes and does calculations is a(n) _mathematician_ .

2 A person who controls the making of something in a factory is a(n) _____ .

3 A person who studies rocks, soils, and minerals and how they have changed over time is a(n) _____ .

4 A person who is the first to think of an idea for a new product and then designs or makes it is a(n) _____ .

5 A person who makes, or repairs, modern machines and equipment, like computers, is a(n) _____ .

6 A person who studies the structure of things like acids and liquids and mixes them in a laboratory is a(n) _____ .

7 A person who studies natural forces, such as light, heat, and movement – and black holes in space is a(n) _____ .

8 A person who studies the movement of the stars and planets is a(n) _____ .

2 Identify the objects in the pictures.

A

_____

B

_____

C

_____

D

_____

E

_____

F

_____

3 Choose the correct answer, A, B, C or D.

1 Now take the _____ and weigh the rock you have chosen.
   A beaker   B test tube
   (C) scales   D thermometer

2 The laboratory _____ we do in our normal science classes are sometimes quite dangerous.
   A experiences   B trials
   C examinations D experiments

3 Our lab assistant had to _____ over the experiment because our teacher was feeling ill.
   A get   B take
   C carry   D come

4 Our _____ is just one of the many groups of stars that make up the universe.
   A planet   B star
   C galaxy   D world

5 Clare's very _____ of how she behaved in our science class yesterday.
   A embarrassed   B sorry
   C apologetic   D ashamed

6 Jessica _____ on washing all the test tubes by herself.
   A stressed   B insisted
   C determined   D wanted

7 Ben's school can't build a new lab because it's suffering from a _____ of cash.
   A lack   B gap
   C space   D loss

8 My dad thinks I'd _____ from extra biology lessons.
   A benefit   B succeed
   C advance   D progress

4 Complete the words in the sentences.

1 Some people believe they've seen flying saucers, but I find the whole idea completely i_n_c_r_ed_i_b_l_e_.

2 If you're really interested in how rocks are formed, you should think about becoming a g_____l_____i_____ .

3 It's very _____l_____y that people will be living on Mars any time soon.

4 Can you pour the liquid into that _____a_____r?

5 Sadly, some of the p_____d_____ scientists make may never come true.

6 Without the force of _____v_____ , objects wouldn't fall to the ground.

5 **Rewrite the sentences, using the word in capitals. Do not use more than five words.**

1 The satellite will travel thousands of kilometres before it goes into orbit.
TRAVELLED
By the time the satellite goes into orbit, *it will have travelled* thousands of kilometres.

2 The demonstration will start very soon.
ABOUT
The demonstration _____.

3 The movie will finish before you get there.
HAVE
By the time you get there, _____.

4 The invention probably won't go on sale.
UNLIKELY
The invention _____ go on sale.

5 What is the departure time for the plane tomorrow?
DOES
What _____ tomorrow?

6 According to this leaflet, the museum should open in ten minutes' time.
DUE
According to this leaflet, the museum _____ in ten minutes' time.

6 **Complete the text with one word in each space.**

Danger from Space!

Over the years there have been many predictions 1) ___*about*___ our planet, Earth. According to some Hollywood movies, a near-Earth object, like an asteroid or a comet, 2) _____ likely to collide with the Earth one day soon. Relax! No asteroids are 3) _____ to hit the Earth – well, not 4) _____ the next few decades anyway. However, over coming years NASA scientists will 5) _____ working on a plan to deal with any such dangers. They hope that by the end of their project, they will 6) _____ worked out how to change the orbit of any asteroid that threatens our planet. During the project, they 7) _____ be thinking about how to put an early warning system in place. Then, if the asteroid is small enough, they may be able to send 8) _____ robotic spacecraft into space to alter its course.

7 **Use the clues to complete the crossword.**

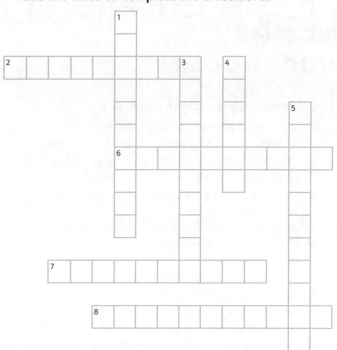

Across
2 A machine that circles the Earth and helps us predict the weather
6 A scientist who studies the stars and the planets
7 A statement about what may happen in the future
8 You use this to measure the temperature.

Down
1 You use this to work out the answer to your multiplication problem.
3 The name given to a scientific test done in a laboratory
4 The name given to creatures from another world
5 A word that means *filled with too many people or things*

O4 Dream jobs

VOCABULARY

1 Choose the correct answer A, B or C.

1 My uncle works in a department _____ .
   A shop   (B) store   C showroom
2 Our local factory is trying to _____ new staff.
   A recruit   B rent   C gain
3 Don't worry! The company will train you in the _____ you need for the job.
   A qualifications B duties   C skills
4 Our teacher is applying for the _____ of headmaster in another school.
   A contract   B post   C work
5 Bob isn't a qualified workman yet; he's an _____ , so he gets training while he works.
   A assistant   B applicant   C apprentice
6 They only _____ Jack last month and now they've dismissed him!
   A hired   B rented   C featured
7 Make sure you read the _____ carefully before you agree to sign it.
   A post   B contract   C application
8 Dad's job involves going round to clients and _____ the company's new projects to them.
   A recruiting   B featuring   C promoting

2 Complete the sentences with these verbs in the appropriate form.

> be made   conduct   earn   fit
> ~~manufacture~~   write

1 I've got a summer job with a company that _manufactures_ cars.
2 I hope my headmaster has _____ me a really good reference.
3 We _____ a survey in class yesterday to find out which jobs are the most popular.
4 My brother won't tell me how much he _____ per month in his job.
5 I thought I'd found my friend a job, but she says she doesn't _____ the job description.
6 My aunt has just _____ redundant.

3 Complete the words in the sentences.

1 If you've always known what career you want, they you have a v _o c a_ t _i o n_ .
2 An official agreement between two or more people. c_____t
3 Doctors are people who make a c_____ out of medicine.
4 If you want a job, you need to fill in this _____p_____t_____form.
5 The people who form most of the staff of a company are the e_____e_____ .
6 They've taken my brother on as an a_____t_____in a local carpentry business.
7 It's easier to find a good job if your head teacher writes you an excellent r_____r_____ .
8 They're reducing the number of staff, so a lot of workers are going to be made r_d_____t.

4 Choose the correct word.

1 My brother's relying *in/by/on* Dad to get him to work on time.
2 Thousands of companies are closing down, so many people are *from/out of/under* work.
3 The cashier charged the customer the wrong amount *in/from/by* mistake.
4 Students are *under/in/on* a lot of pressure to acquire good job skills these days.
5 We're not allowed to ring Mum *at/in/on* work because it disturbs her too much.
6 You'll be *on/for/in* trouble with the boss if you come to work late.
7 Make sure you arrive *on/in/at* time for the planning meeting!
8 Dad says he's been *on/under/in* his feet all day and he needs to sit down.

5 Use the clues to complete the crossword.

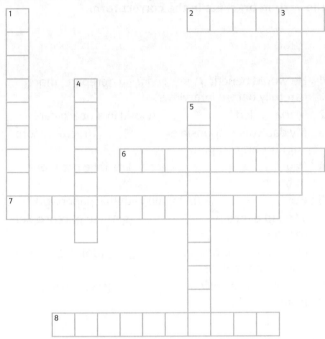

Across

2 If a policeman arrests you, you may need help from this person.

6 A person who is willing to work for no money

7 A person who checks people in and out of a hotel

8 If your business needs help dealing with finance, ask this person.

Down

1 A person who tells us about the news on the TV

3 A person or company that pays people to do a job

4 You may go to this person for special advice.

5 A person who writes for a newspaper

6 Complete the table.

	Noun	Verb	Adjective
1	demand	demand	*demanding*
2	xxxxx	flex	
3	idiot	xxxxx	
4	practice	practise	
5	competition	compete	
6	knowledge	know	
7	motivation	motivate	
8	sense	xxxxx	/sensitive

7 Complete the sentences by changing the words in capitals into adjectives.

1 We were hoping to repair the machine, but the damage is not __*reversible*__ .   REVERSE

2 It's _____ to spend time with a careers adviser before you choose your career.   SENSE

3 What you did was completely _____ . IDIOT

4 Terry must be telling lies; his excuse is completely _____ .   BELIEVE

5 Saving lives as a doctor must be really _____ .   SATISFY

6 A job in a factory can be quite _____ .   REPEAT

7 If your job involves being on your feet all day, it must be so _____ .   TIRE

8 Technologists have to be quite _____ these days.   INVENT

8 Complete the article with the correct form of the word in capitals.

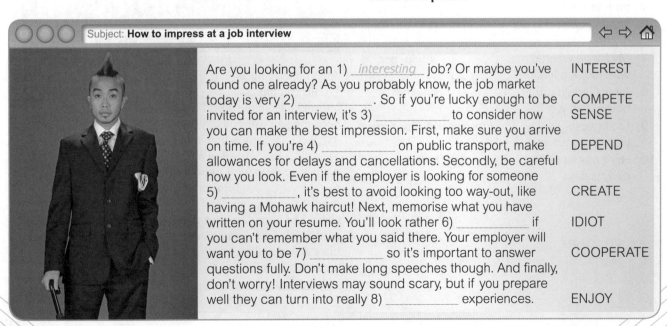

Subject: **How to impress at a job interview**

Are you looking for an 1) __*interesting*__ job? Or maybe you've found one already? As you probably know, the job market today is very 2) _____ . So if you're lucky enough to be invited for an interview, it's 3) _____ to consider how you can make the best impression. First, make sure you arrive on time. If you're 4) _____ on public transport, make allowances for delays and cancellations. Secondly, be careful how you look. Even if the employer is looking for someone 5) _____ , it's best to avoid looking too way-out, like having a Mohawk haircut! Next, memorise what you have written on your resume. You'll look rather 6) _____ if you can't remember what you said there. Your employer will want you to be 7) _____ so it's important to answer questions fully. Don't make long speeches though. And finally, don't worry! Interviews may sound scary, but if you prepare well they can turn into really 8) _____ experiences.

INTEREST

COMPETE

SENSE

DEPEND

CREATE

IDIOT

COOPERATE

ENJOY

GRAMMAR
Grammar focus: gerunds and infinitives

1 Choose the correct form of the verb.

1 I've decided *studying/study/to study* law when I leave school.

2 It's not worth *apply/applying/to apply* for that job because it doesn't pay well.

3 *Nurse/To nurse/Nursing* is a great vocation.

4 My sister's job involves *promote/promoting/to promote* beauty products.

5 My mum doesn't want me *leave/to leave/leaving* home for good.

6 I intend to spend a year *travel/travelling/to travel* before I go to university.

7 Do you happen *to know/knowing/know* what the salary is?

8 Dad's boss made him *to work/work/working* overtime last week.

2 Complete the sentences with the verbs in brackets in the correct form.

1 Have you considered _____*taking*_____ (take) a temporary job?

2 I didn't intend _____ (annoy) you.

3 I'm looking forward to _____ (hear) from the company.

4 His dad made him _____ (cut) his hair before the interview.

5 Did you manage _____ (change) the time of the interview?

6 I hope I don't end up _____ (be) late for my first day.

7 My friend wanted me _____ (help) her with her application.

8 James would rather _____ (stay) at home than work.

9 I'd suggest _____ (not/wear) those torn jeans for your interview!

10 Her boss let her _____ (go) home early today.

3 Complete the sentences with a preposition and put the verb in brackets in the correct form.

> about   for   ~~from~~   in x2   on   up   with

1 He would benefit _*from preparing*_ (prepare) more carefully before interviews.

2 Maria ended _____ (work) in a beach café.

3 My dad was responsible _____ (recruit) more staff for his company.

4 Paul insists _____ (stay) late if he has work to finish.

5 How _____ (help) me with this paperwork?

6 We had difficulty _____ (get) the photocopier to work.

7 Nurses have to put up _____ (do) shift work even if they hate it.

8 I'd like to be involved _____ (save) animals from extinction.

4 Complete the text with one word in each space.

A Job with a Difference

Are you looking 1) _*forward*_ to leaving school? Would you like 2) _____ do one of the most unusual jobs in the world? Well, how 3) _____ becoming an ostrich babysitter? You won't be 4) _____ too much pressure – you just 5) _____ to sit in a field full of ostriches and make sure they don't fight! Or perhaps you'd prefer to 6) _____ a furniture tester? For this job, all you need to do while you're 7) _____ work is to test chairs and beds - by sitting or lying on them! It's the perfect job for a couch potato – you know, someone who likes sitting and watching TV all the time – and so much nicer than being 8) _____ your feet all day!

Grammar focus: verb patterns

5 **Complete each pair of sentences with the correct form of the verb in capitals.**

1 TAKE

   A: Oh no! I forgot _to take_ our dinner out of the freezer!

   B: I'll never forget _taking_ my boss's phone home by mistake. How embarrassing!

2 SPEAK

   A: The manager stopped _____ when Dad's mobile phone rang.

   B: The manager stopped _____ to a technician about the problem.

3 GET

   A: We tried _____ an interview with the TV presenter, but without success.

   B: If your computer won't let you access the Internet, try _____ a new router.

4 PHONE

   A: Did you remember _____ the company manager?

   B: I can't remember _____ the repair shop, but I'm sure I did.

5 GET

   A: I like _____ together with friends. We always have fun together.

   B: Our teacher likes us _____ to class early.

6 **Make correct sentences from the prompts.**

1 I / try / tell my boss about the problem but I / not able / find him.

   I tried to tell my boss about the problem but I wasn't able to find him.

2 Only yesterday, the manager / warn / staff / not touch / the broken switch.

3 He / stop / work at the factory when he / get / a better job.

4 My last teacher / always / encourage me / work hard.

5 Please / not expect me / work / evenings.

6 I / not remember / the boss / tell me that / but I suppose he did.

7 **Identify the five sentences which contain a mistake and correct them.**

1 Did you remember posting my letter as I requested? ✗

   Did you remember to post my letter as I requested?

2 We stopped getting more petrol as we had nearly run out of fuel.

3 If your computer develops a problem, try switching it off and then on again.

4 Can you remember to suck your thumb when you were younger?

5 Please don't encourage George misbehaving.

6 I really wish I could stop to bite my nails. It's an awful habit!

7 I'm trying to ring Sarah but I can't get a signal.

8 You must remind me paying you the money I owe you.

8 **Rewrite the sentences using the words in capitals. Use between two and five words, including the word given.**

1 Trips to the cinema are enjoyable.

   LIKE

   I _like going to_ the cinema.

2 I must continue to save for my holidays.

   STOP

   I must not _____ for my holidays.

3 Barbara is certain that she put the keys on the table.

   REMEMBERS

   Barbara _____ on the table.

4 Mum texted to say I shouldn't be late for my interview.

   REMINDED

   Mum _____ late for my interview.

5 Tom's boss said he must continue without taking a break.

   STOP

   Tom's boss said he couldn't _____ .

6 Her train was late so she couldn't get to work on time.

   TRIED

   She _____ work on time, but she couldn't because her train was late.

Revision Unit 4

1 Choose the correct answer, A, B or C.

1 The boys stripped _____ their clothes and jumped in the river.
   A out   **B** off   C down

2 If the store closes down, all the staff will be _____ redundant.
   A found   B made   C kept

3 I enjoy having a _____ every morning during the holidays.
   A sleep-in   B stay-in   C lie-in

4 My dad always encourages me to _____ high in life.
   A aim   B shoot   C fire

5 Emma is extremely _____ so she would make great speeches as a politician.
   A attractive   B winning   C articulate

6 The producer left no _____ unturned in his search for a leading lady.
   A stone   B rock   C pebble

7 Standing under a tree when there is lightning about is crazy and could _____ you in hospital.
   A finish   B land   C end

8 Working every day of the week is not my _____ of heaven!
   A version   B idea   C dream

2 Find ten words on the topic of work. The words go across, down or diagonally. The first letter of each word is highlighted.

r	m	b	o	c	o	n	t	r	a	c	t	c	r	c
r	e	f	e	r	e	n	c	e	y	v	m	o	s	l
p	j	k	r	e	c	r	u	i	t	d	z	n	d	j
o	w	z	o	c	y	t	x	s	i	j	o	s	t	f
b	e	f	z	e	k	w	p	t	s	i	c	e	e	k
r	i	s	e	p	e	g	e	j	t	a	a	r	p	n
v	o	t	j	t	n	h	b	a	g	d	l	v	v	t
n	d	a	h	i	p	f	c	u	s	l	e	a	c	v
i	q	f	l	o	l	i	v	u	l	e	x	t	r	g
u	x	f	d	n	f	a	q	m	y	a	g	i	s	y
m	i	w	l	i	o	e	w	o	c	x	i	o	u	x
s	i	l	l	s	p	t	l	y	b	a	p	n	l	b
x	m	a	z	t	t	p	z	v	e	z	n	i	m	p
c	u	h	c	u	m	q	o	j	o	r	o	q	c	s
q	o	i	k	e	d	r	e	d	u	n	d	a	n	t

3 Complete the sentences with the correct form of the word in capitals.

1 All the _employees_ who work in the mines have to wear hard hats because the job is so dangerous. **EMPLOY**

2 Did the head teacher write you a good job _____? **REFER**

3 You need to list your _____ on the form they sent you. **QUALIFY**

4 The _____ with the best skill set got the only job. **APPLY**

5 It's hard to find a job these days, so it helps if you're _____. **COMPETE**

6 Fiona's not very _____; in fact, she spends all her time dreaming! **PRACTICE**

7 Let me know if you see a _____ job for me when you're on the Internet. **SUIT**

8 My teacher's really _____ about the careers I can choose. **KNOWLEDGE**

4 Match words from each list to make logical collocations.

1 get — j a new job
2 be made   a a contract
3 conduct   b a new skill
4 earn   c a product
5 fill in   d a role
6 learn   e a salary
7 manufacture   f an application form
8 play   g a survey
9 recruit   h redundant
10 sign   i staff
                   j a new job

5 Complete the sentences by putting the verbs in brackets into the correct form.

1 My interests include drama and _reading_. (read)

2 I'm interested in _____ (know) what qualifications you need to be a vet.

3 Her mum stopped her from _____ (get) a summer job.

4 Dan promised _____ (help) me fill in my application form.

5 My dad's job involves _____ (meet) lots of people.

6 We happened _____ (see) the company director in the street yesterday.

6 Rewrite the sentences using the words in capitals. Use between two and five words, including the word given.

1 There's no alternative to working long hours. **PUT**
We have to *put up with working* long hours.

2 My employer wouldn't give me permission to leave work early. **LET**
My employer _____ work early.

3 Jon is not accustomed to doing shift work. **USED**
John _____ shift work.

4 The staff were keen on me making a speech at the meeting. **WANTED**
The staff _____ a speech at the meeting.

5 It might be a good idea to get some work experience before you decide on your future career. **SUGGEST**
I _____ work experience before you decide on your future career.

6 Applying for a job without the necessary skills is a waste of time. **WORTH**
It _____ a job if you don't have the necessary skills.

7 The careers adviser didn't keep me waiting for too long, thank goodness. **MAKE**
Thank goodness the careers adviser didn't _____ too long.

8 Do you fancy going to a movie after work? **ABOUT**
How _____ after work?

7 Complete the text with the best answer, A, B, C or D.

	A		B		C		D
1	A	any	B	no	C	some	D	few
2	A	wish	B	ambition	C	vocation	D	intention
3	A	allow	B	permit	C	enable	D	let
4	A	in	B	at	C	on	D	from
5	A	before	B	for	C	under	D	over
6	A	on	B	with	C	onto	D	by
7	A	succeeds	B	endures	C	intends	D	manages
8	A	ends	B	comes	C	brings	D	takes

(1 B is circled)

A Rewarding Career

I have 1) _____ idea what to do when I leave school. I envy people who know exactly what career they want to follow from an early age. If you have a definite 2) _____ – for the religious life, for example, or for nursing – that must be great. My mum always wanted to be a nurse because it was a job that would 3) _____ her help others. She works in a busy emergency department so she sees people who are 4) _____ all sorts of trouble. This means she is 5) _____ a lot of pressure all day. She's 6) _____ her feet all day, too – she must walk several kilometres every week! I don't know how she 7) _____ to keep going, but she does - and she never complains, either! Nurses can retire at the age of sixty in my country, but I bet Mum 8) _____ up working until she's seventy.

8 Complete the conversation with the correct form of these verbs.

> be   do   find   ~~go~~   not/worry
> phone   walk   work

Sam: How was your work experience interview, Ann?

Ann: Getting there was the worst bit. We'd planned 1) *to go* by bus, but there was a strike.

Sam: Oh no! Did you end up 2) _____ all the way?

Ann: No, thank goodness. We managed 3) _____ a taxi. It cost a fortune, though!

Sam: Oh! Well, you couldn't help 4) _____ late in that case.

Ann: No, and luckily the boss was lovely and told me 5) _____ .

Sam: And how did things go after that?

Ann: It was great. They asked me all the usual questions, like what job I want 6) _____ when I leave school and whether I've ever had experience of 7) _____ in a shop before. They seemed really interested and they've promised 8) _____ me later to say when I can start!

Sam: Brilliant! Well done, Ann!

VOCABULARY

1 Choose the correct answer, A, B, or C.

1 The two boys glared at each other angrily, then clenched their _____ and started to box.
A ankles
B fists
C wrists

2 You won't be very healthy if you insist on eating _____ food.
A rotten
B waste
C junk

3 Last night I _____ downstairs, careful not to wake my parents, and stepped outside into the moonlit street.
A sneaked
B rushed
C bumped

4 When mum saw what my little brother had been _____ while she was away, she punished him severely.
A down to
B away with
C up to

5 My dad's a farmer and my eldest brother is hoping to follow in his _____ .
A feet
B shoes
C way

6 One of my friends _____ on Saturday to pick up the tablet she'd lent me.
A dropped by
B went round
C fell in

7 Some people believe girls should be _____ from boxing because it's far too dangerous.
A banned
B finished
C controlled

8 If you're _____ , you will want to beat other people at sport in a fair way.
A big-headed
B competitive
C aggressive

2 Choose the word in each list that does not fit in with the others.

1 double fault   foul   win
2 ace   chalk   knockout
3 spar   champion   opponent
4 umpire   referee   coach
5 dribble   serve   ring
6 net   fist   goalpost
7 pitch   court   punch

3 Complete the text with the best answer, A, B, C or D.

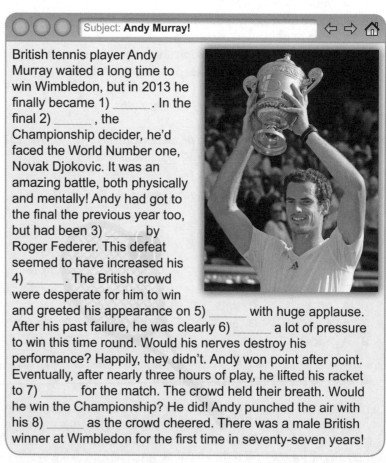

Subject: **Andy Murray!**

British tennis player Andy Murray waited a long time to win Wimbledon, but in 2013 he finally became 1) _____ . In the final 2) _____ , the Championship decider, he'd faced the World Number one, Novak Djokovic. It was an amazing battle, both physically and mentally! Andy had got to the final the previous year too, but had been 3) _____ by Roger Federer. This defeat seemed to have increased his 4) _____ . The British crowd were desperate for him to win and greeted his appearance on 5) _____ with huge applause. After his past failure, he was clearly 6) _____ a lot of pressure to win this time round. Would his nerves destroy his performance? Happily, they didn't. Andy won point after point. Eventually, after nearly three hours of play, he lifted his racket to 7) _____ for the match. The crowd held their breath. Would he win the Championship? He did! Andy punched the air with his 8) _____ as the crowd cheered. There was a male British winner at Wimbledon for the first time in seventy-seven years!

1 A competitor **B** player **C** champion **D** rival
2 A fight **B** match **C** play **D** competition
3 A won **B** caught **C** beaten **D** taken
4 A motivation **B** expectation **C** competition **D** inclination
5 A ring **B** field **C** pitch **D** court
6 A in **B** below **C** under **D** on
7 A dribble **B** serve **C** shot **D** stroke
8 A head **B** knee **C** fist **D** wrist

4 Complete the sentences with these words.

> do   give   have   make
> miss   run   ~~score~~   take

1 The crowd cheered when the local team managed to ___score___ a goal.
2 I'm doing my best so please _____ me a break!
3 If you play rugby, you _____ the risk of getting badly injured.
4 The United player was unfortunate enough to _____ a penalty, which meant the team lost the game.
5 If you're a top tennis player, you can _____ a fortune at Wimbledon.
6 Going to dance classes will really _____ you good!
7 If you don't _____ any notice of what the referee says, you'll be sent off the field!
8 To be a champion, you need to _____ a lot of confidence in your skills.

5 Find ten words on the topic of sport. The words go across, down or diagonally. The first letter of each word is highlighted.

m	o	s	o	n	e	n	b	u	o	a	s	b	r	v
c	e	e	t	v	q	v	m	m	w	x	c	z	s	b
o	t	r	y	m	q	a	z	p	z	g	d	a	g	c
u	j	v	a	e	y	p	s	i	z	h	i	v	o	r
r	c	e	n	c	k	p	z	r	b	l	w	s	a	p
t	n	y	i	j	k	r	i	e	k	x	b	h	l	i
r	e	f	e	r	e	e	n	t	x	y	h	w	m	h
r	a	f	o	s	e	n	t	b	c	i	e	x	f	t
a	c	c	o	u	n	t	a	n	t	h	w	d	l	q
y	j	f	n	u	o	i	g	x	z	r	n	n	a	l
r	k	a	n	y	l	c	o	u	j	r	a	h	q	z
w	h	a	g	e	m	e	l	f	d	i	v	i	n	g
e	b	o	n	i	k	h	b	o	x	i	n	g	k	d
x	d	g	b	m	u	c	l	m	t	n	b	c	v	e
s	a	n	d	o	p	v	h	z	y	b	g	r	l	d

6 Choose the correct word.

1 The rugby captain was ill so my brother stood *to/up/in* for him.
2 Most referees won't put up *for/with/by* bad behaviour.
3 Five members of the team have gone *up/down/out* with 'flu!
4 I wish they'd do *in/off/away* with some football rules because I find them confusing.
5 Sadly, our side ran *away with/out of/by from* energy halfway through the game.
6 He scored a goal, which made *in/out/up* for his previous mistake.

7 Match a preposition with a verb to complete a phrasal verbs and its meaning.

> along with   do with   down on
> in for   out of   ~~forward to~~

1 to look forward ___to___ = to anticipate something with pleasure
2 to look _____ = to treat someone as if they are inferior to you
3 to make _____ = to manage with what you've got
4 to run _____ = to have no more left of something
5 to stand _____ = to temporarily replace someone
6 to go _____ = to agree with an idea or suggestion

8 Choose the correct answer, A, B or C.

1 You have to _____ with the rules even if you disagree with them.
   A take on   B go along   C come up
2 Some people criticised the captain, but I _____ up for him.
   A took   B got   C stood
3 I think all schools should do _____ all compulsory sport.
   A away with   B out of   C along with
4 You shouldn't _____ on somebody just because they're not sporty.
   A bring down   B come up   C look down
5 I don't go _____ girls doing boxing.
   A along with   B in for   C up with
6 If you haven't got your own boots, you'll have to make _____ these.
   A out with   B do with   C up for

GRAMMAR
Grammar focus: the conditional

1 **Choose the correct form of the verb.**

1 If there *will/would be/are* any tickets left for the match, I'll buy some.

2 If I *wouldn't be/weren't/won't be* so lazy, *I'd go/ I went* for a swim.

3 You'll get fat unless you *take/don't take/will take/ won't take* more exercise.

4 *We go/We'll go* skateboarding tomorrow if the sun *will shine/is shining*.

5 When I *got/get/will get* home, I *look/'ll look* for my tennis racket.

6 Take your camera in case *you'll see/you see/you saw* a celebrity at the arena.

7 If my dad *didn't/wouldn't* work with athletes, I *didn't/wouldn't/don't* meet them so often.

8 I'm not going to the pitch with you unless you *let/ will let* me play.

9 If you *were/would be* offered tickets for a World Cup football match, *would/will* you go?

10 That footballer *never plays/will never play* well unless he *gets/will get* more training.

2 **Cross out the one unnecessary word in each sentence.**

1 Don't bang that racket on the ground in case you ~~will~~ break it.

2 Unless I would play better, the coach will not pick me for the team.

3 We can go out cycling provided if we are back for lunch.

4 Do ring me if you will decide to go to the match.

5 If I would had more money, I would be able to buy more trainers.

6 Take an umbrella in the case it rains.

7 I could go to football practice when I am able to.

8 I could book a court if I would knew how much it costs.

3 **Complete the sentences using the prompts.**

1 If my brother / win / the championship / tomorrow, he may go professional.
If my brother wins the championship tomorrow, he may go professional.

2 We / not / join / the local gym tonight / unless / it / be /cheap.

3 Jan / always / win / when I / play / her at tennis, but I'm hoping to change that soon.

4 They / cancel / the final / if the champion / be / ill, but luckily he was fine.

5 I / take / my football boots with me today in case the trainer / ask me to play. I hope so!

6 I / serve / better in the game last week if I / not injure / my shoulder.

4 **Rewrite the sentences using the words in capitals. Use between two and five words, including the word given.**

1 I don't think you should dive from that rock. WERE
If I *were you, I wouldn't* dive from that rock.

2 She's not getting a new bicycle because she can't afford it.   IF
She would get a new bicycle _____ it.

3 I won't go bowling without you.   UNLESS
I won't go bowling _____ .

4 She played netball because her friend asked her to.   NOT
She wouldn't have played netball if her friend _____ to.

5 Concentrate hard, and you'll win the match.   YOU
You'll win the match if _____ .

6 There's a chance you may fall off your horse, so wear a helmet.   CASE
Wear a helmet _____ your horse.

7 He hurt his leg so he lost the race.   MIGHT
If he hadn't hurt his leg, he _____ the race.

5 Complete the text with an appropriate word in each space. Use any word once only.

Teenage Food Champions

Tanya is 1) _____a_____ brilliant teenage chef. She 2) _____ never have started cooking if her dad hadn't fallen ill last year. Her mum works long hours in her job, so there's nobody to put dinner on the table 3) _____ Tanya takes over the cooking. There are ready meals waiting in the freezer just in 4) _____ Tanya's efforts end in disaster. But they rarely do! She grows her own salad vegetables, so provided it 5) _____ the right season she has fresh ingredients to use in her food. If she 6) _____ not have much time, she makes pasta or pizza, but she's usually more ambitious than that. She's grateful to her home economics teacher. 'If she 7) _____ not helped me, I wouldn't have had the courage to cook for everybody', she says. So is she really a good cook? Take her brother's word for it when he says, 'If I 8) _____ choose between having a dinner cooked by Tanya and going to a fast food restaurant, I'd choose Tanya's dinner. There's no better recommendation than that!'

Grammar focus: mixed conditionals

6 Complete the sentences by matching the parts.

1 If you didn't eat junk food,

2 If you took more exercise,

3 If you hadn't eaten so many snacks last night,

4 If you had spent less time in the gym,

5 If you hadn't missed the team selection meeting,

6 If you had scored a winning goal,

7 Provided you spend more time training,

8 If you had missed scoring that goal,

a you wouldn't be so popular now.

b you could have made it onto the team.

c you'd be a hero now.

d you wouldn't be so fit now.

e you'd be thinner and healthier.

f you'll reach the top in your sport.

g you could get really fit.

h you might have found it easier to do up your jeans this morning.

7 Choose the correct answer, A, B or C.

1 If I _____ more in the past, I'd be better at tennis now.
   - **A** had practised
   - **B** practised
   - **C** was practising

2 My sister _____ a ballet dancer if she weren't so tall.
   - **A** could become
   - **B** could be becoming
   - **C** could have become

3 If there weren't a café near our school, we _____ at all yesterday.
   - **A** mightn't have eaten
   - **B** mightn't eat
   - **C** mightn't have been eating

4 If I _____ to the gym more often last year, I'd be fitter now.
   - **A** went
   - **B** had gone
   - **C** was going

5 If I _____ to bed earlier last night, I'd feel more like taking part in Sports Day today!
   - **A** would have gone
   - **B** went
   - **C** had gone

6 We wouldn't have to queue now if _____ to book a table in advance.
   - **A** we'd remembered
   - **B** we remembered
   - **C** we'd remember

8 Complete the second sentence so that it means the same as the first.

1 You didn't wash the dishes last night so you have no clean plates this morning.
   But you would _have clean plates this morning if you had washed the dishes last night_ .

2 I can't buy lunch because I left my money at home this morning.
   But if I _____ .

3 I'm only able to cook now because my gran taught me.
   I wouldn't _____ unless _____ .

4 I ate too much so now I'm not able to do up my jeans.
   If I _____ .

5 You're feeling hungry now because you didn't eat breakfast.
   But you _____ .

6 I couldn't meet you earlier because it's my dad's birthday today.
   But if _____ .

Revision Unit 5

1 Choose the correct word.

1 Who's first on the *tennis pitch/ring/court* this morning?
2 If you're competitive, you want to *win/beat/catch* your opponent.
3 The people taking part in a sports event are called *rivals/competitors/champions*.
4 My brother was delighted because he *scored/gained/made* a goal.
5 The footballer was sent off the pitch for committing a *mistake/foul/fault*.
6 The boxer punched the man with his *foot/fist/head*.
7 I'd like to make a pizza, but I haven't got the right *ingredients/menus/foods*.
8 Has she got enough *imagination/intention/motivation* to make her practise night and day to win?

2 Complete the text with one appropriate word in each space. Use any word once only.

Subject: **Sugar Alert!** ⇦ ⇨ ⌂

We all know it's important
1) ___*to*___ take care of our bodies
2) _____ we want to look good and
stay healthy. Playing football or tennis, for
example, isn't just great fun; it
3) _____ do you a lot of good,
as well. Of course you have to watch
your diet, too; 4) _____ you're
careful what you eat, you run the risk of
becoming overweight or getting ill. If you
5) _____ the wrong kinds of food,
you could end up being really moody, too.
Why? Because scientists have discovered
that sugary foods 6) _____
chocolate and biscuits are 'bad mood
foods'. They give you 7) _____
quick burst of energy, but when that
wears off, you may feel irritable and tired.
So, if you 8) _____ feeling grumpy
today, you know what to do – cut out
the sugar!

3 Complete the sentences with the correct preposition.

1 David came ___*up*___ with a brilliant suggestion for next year's competition.
2 I hope you'll stand _____ for me if the referee blames me for the team's poor performance.
3 We don't really understand why the rules have changed, but we're happy to go _____ with them anyway.
4 Has Paul come _____ from his operation yet or is he still unconscious?
5 Mum says she won't put up _____ us leaving our muddy boots around any more!
6 I'm sorry I let you down, but I promise I'll make up _____ it in another way.
7 The captain comes _____ with some amazing jokes in the changing rooms.
8 I don't get _____ with my trainer at all.

4 Complete the text with the best answer, A, B, C or D.

1 **A** information   **(B)** skill

Daredevils!

Extreme sports usually require a
great deal of 1) _____, so the
people who 2) _____ part in the
activities need to 3) _____ a lot
of confidence in themselves. If
they don't stay in control of their
actions, they run the 4) _____ of
hurting themselves really badly.
There are no 5) _____ to obey in
most of these sports.
Participants don't usually join
together in 6) _____ either, as they do in football or
cricket, for example. Extreme sports can be very
dangerous! Street skaters, for example, are always
coming 7) _____ with new and even more incredible
places to do tricks. If you're interested in extreme sports,
I 8) _____ definitely advise you to join a club.

	C knowledge		**D** information	
2 **A** have	**B** do	**C** take	**D** want
3 **A** contain	**B** believe	**C** leave	**D** have
4 **A** risk	**B** opportunity	**C** hope	**D** chance
5 **A** laws	**B** rules	**C** commands	**D** duties
6 **A** teams	**B** sides	**C** lines	**D** rows
7 **A** in	**B** down	**C** over	**D** up
8 **A** will	**B** shall	**C** would	**D** did

5 Complete the words in the sentences.

1 After my main course I had a huge ice cream for d _e_ _s_ _s_ _e_ _r_ _t_ .

2 I broke my leg so I had to go into hospital for an o_____ at_____ .

3 Because I hadn't eaten all day I felt very weak and eventually I f_____nt_____ .

4 I'm starving hungry! What's on the m_____u for dinner tonight?

5 If you're c___mp___t_____e, you're determined to be better than other people.

6 If you have m_____v__t_____n, you are keen and willing to do something.

7 You put a s___d_____e on a horse before you ride it.

8 I'm trying to diet, but I find sugary foods are a terrible t___mp_____n.

6 Rewrite the words using the sentences in capitals. Use between two and five words, including the word given.

1 My advice is to get more swimming lessons.
YOU
If I _were you, I would get_ more swimming lessons.

2 I didn't go to the training so I'm not in the team now.
I
I could be in the team now if _____ the training.

3 He wasn't able to go swimming because he forgot his swimming things.
COULD
He _____ if he'd remembered his swimming things.

4 I broke my leg last month so I can't go skiing this year.
NOT
If I _____ my leg last month, I could go skiing this year.

5 I'm only asking for extra coaching because I need it.
UNLESS
I wouldn't ask for extra coaching _____ .

6 You live a long way from green fields so you can't keep a horse.
NEARER
If _____ to green fields, you could keep a horse.

7 It might be hot so take some sun cream.
CASE
Take some sun cream _____ hot.

7 Find the mistake in each of these sentences and correct it.

1 If I won't practise tennis every day, I forget how to hit the ball properly.
If I don't practise tennis every day, I forget how to hit the ball properly.

2 I'll buy a ticket for the boxing contest, but when I can't get there in time, you go in without me.

3 You won't be able to play football if you will forget your boots.

4 I bring your cycle helmet in case you need it, shall I?

5 I'd be careful when doing extreme sports if I'd be you.

6 If I won't see you in the gym, I'll text you.

7 Provided it won't rain tomorrow, we can play the game outdoors.

8 I won't sell you these trainers unless you don't pay me immediately.

8 Use the clues to complete the crossword.

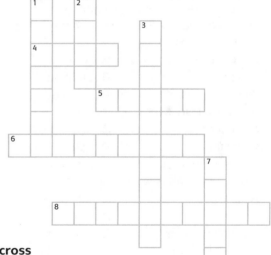

Across

4 You close your hand and make this if you are going to punch someone.

5 A verb meaning to play in a dishonest way in order to win

6 An adjective used to describe food that tastes really good

8 Something you want to have or do even though you know you should not

Down

1 Someone who makes sure that the rules of a sport like football are obeyed

2 An adjective to describe food which is prepared quickly and that you can take away

3 This phrasal verb means _manage with what you've got_.

7 An adjective to describe food that is very hot and peppery, like Indian food

06 showtime

VOCABULARY

1 Choose the correct answer, A, B, C or D.

1 Our school deals very severely with incidents of bullying and _____ .
   A naming
   B labelling
   C nicknaming
   (D) name-calling

2 I can't come out tonight because I've got to learn my _____ for the school play tonight.
   A plays
   B lines
   C notes
   D orders

3 I'd much rather go to a _____ performance of a play than a pre-recorded one.
   A living
   B lively
   C live
   D lifetime

4 To get a part in the musical I had to _____ in front of the director, along with fifty other hopeful actors!
   A rehearse
   B react
   C play
   D audition

5 You need a lot of _____ if you're going to become a lead actor in a film.
   A culture
   B art
   C talent
   D gifts

6 Tom missed two _____ for the play so the director gave his role to someone else.
   A practices
   B meetings
   C acts
   D rehearsals

7 My grandparents _____ so they could get married in secret.
   A departed
   B migrated
   C eloped
   D disobeyed

8 I'll describe the _____ of the film, but I won't give away the ending in case I spoil it for you.
   A plot
   B story
   C event
   D summary

9 Clare wanted the lead role, but she's ended up playing quite a minor _____ instead.
   A person
   B character
   C actor
   D individual

10 My mum has offered to help make the _____ I'll be wearing in the play.
   A robe
   B apparel
   C clothing
   D costume

2 Complete the sentences with these words in the correct form.

| blame | challenge | confess | ~~insult~~ | loathe |
| mix | quit | struggle | | |

1 Bullies often ___*insult*___ people and call them names.

2 Last week, my best friend _____ me to enter the singing competition.

3 I have always _____ horror films – I just think they're rubbish!

4 The director kept criticising me in rehearsals, so in the end I _____ .

5 Record producers often _____ different sounds together to create a music album.

6 I have a bad memory so I always have to _____ to learn my lines.

7 The director _____ himself when the play did badly at the box office.

8 Jessica _____ last night that she'd stolen some jewellery from the dressing room.

3 Choose the correct answer, A, B or C.

1 Keep quiet about the party because we don't want people to _____ it!
   A doorstep
   B footpath
   (C) gate-crash

2 When Romeo and Juliet meet, it is a case of love at first _____ .
   A look
   B sight
   C glance

3 Dan's got so many _____ , I think he should see a psychiatrist!
   A hang-ups
   B pin-ups
   C turn-ups

4 In the play, the teenagers get angry and refuse to listen to their parents. Does that _____ any bells with you?
   A sound
   B play
   C ring

5 I'm not sure if Peter will make a good actor, but time will _____ .
   A speak
   B say
   C tell

6 In summer, I often _____ at the beach with my friends.
   A hang up
   B hang out
   C hang down

7 I've had an awful day - everything I've done has gone _____ !
   A wrong
   B bad
   C false

4 Choose the correct word.

1. I wanted to act in the play, but I ended *out/off/up* building the set!
2. I arranged to meet a friend at the cinema, but he didn't show *down/round/up*.
3. Our local drama club are hoping to put *up/on/in* a musical this year.
4. Can you hang *on/up/by* a minute while I answer this phone call?
5. Sarah is really bitchy; she's always running people *over/through/down*.
6. If you mess *out/over/around* in class, you'll get into trouble!
7. We need to check *over/by/out* what time the gig starts before we plan our evening.
8. You'll need to set *in/off/up* early if you want good seats for the performance.

5 Complete the table below.

	Verb or adjective	Noun
1	fly	*flight*
2	long	
3	think	
4	grieve	
5	see	
6	die	
7	confess	
8	young	
9	weigh	
10	broad	

6 Find ten words on the topic of the arts. The words go across, down or diagonally. The first letter of each word is highlighted.

m	j	h	p	x	g	h	w	y	k	z	a	l	p	h
l	a	r	r	e	q	t	t	n	p	b	m	z	x	n
m	w	u	y	o	p	b	p	h	y	d	q	b	y	f
t	t	l	s	n	z	t	i	m	a	k	e	u	p	g
p	a	d	w	v	d	c	x	v	z	e	t	x	z	e
e	s	l	p	r	e	h	e	a	r	s	a	l	q	b
z	e	u	e	d	j	a	e	q	t	t	f	t	e	c
m	t	d	x	n	j	r	j	x	x	f	g	p	z	o
t	k	i	q	o	t	a	u	d	i	t	i	o	n	s
c	p	r	l	q	r	c	u	t	c	c	n	f	m	t
h	i	e	p	l	o	t	d	a	e	u	r	p	j	u
c	b	c	d	f	i	e	w	r	g	i	t	r	s	m
p	p	t	f	p	e	r	f	o	r	m	a	n	c	e
s	o	o	a	w	t	b	b	e	c	o	l	o	g	y
v	z	r	q	q	n	l	s	f	e	j	j	v	z	o

7 Complete the sentences with the correct form of the word in capitals.

1. Can you guess the ___*weight*___ of this crown? It's so heavy to wear! **WEIGH**
2. I really tried, but I found it _____ to learn my lines in time for the rehearsal. **POSSIBLE**
3. Katrina is scared to _____ that she'll fall off the stage! **DIE**
4. The guitarist was really nervous, so it was a _____ to hear that the audience were enjoying the concert. **RELIEVE**
5. It must be difficult for actors to portray _____ on the stage. **GRIEVE**
6. Belonging to a dance group is keeping me fit and _____ . **HEALTH**

8 Complete the article with the correct form of the words in capitals.

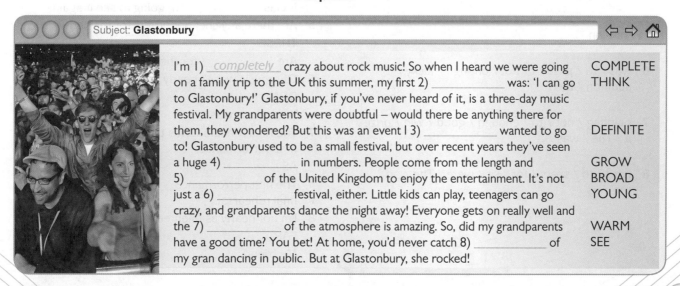

Subject: **Glastonbury**

I'm 1) ___*completely*___ crazy about rock music! So when I heard we were going on a family trip to the UK this summer, my first 2) _____ was: 'I can go to Glastonbury!' Glastonbury, if you've never heard of it, is a three-day music festival. My grandparents were doubtful – would there be anything there for them, they wondered? But this was an event I 3) _____ wanted to go to! Glastonbury used to be a small festival, but over recent years they've seen a huge 4) _____ in numbers. People come from the length and 5) _____ of the United Kingdom to enjoy the entertainment. It's not just a 6) _____ festival, either. Little kids can play, teenagers can go crazy, and grandparents dance the night away! Everyone gets on really well and the 7) _____ of the atmosphere is amazing. So, did my grandparents have a good time? You bet! At home, you'd never catch 8) _____ of my gran dancing in public. But at Glastonbury, she rocked!

COMPLETE
THINK

DEFINITE

GROW
BROAD
YOUNG

WARM
SEE

GRAMMAR
Grammar focus: comparative structures

1 Complete the sentences with a comparative or superlative form of the verb in brackets.

1 Jack was _a lot more nervous_ I thought he'd be. (a lot / nervous)
2 I've just seen the .... rock band in the world. (crazy)
3 The film was .... than I'd expected. (a great deal / entertaining)
4 Colette is .... dancer in our group. (by far / talented)
5 I wasn't .... you were. (nearly/good)
6 The more we rehearse the play, the .... I feel about it. (good)
7 This year we have .... free time than normal. (much/little)
8 My singing is .... than yours! (a great deal / bad)

2 Put the words in the correct order.

1 expensive / us / too / The / were / tickets / for / .
   The tickets were too expensive for us.
2 too / were / learn / lines / difficult / for / him / to / The / .
   ....
3 ground / enough / sit / The / was / comfortable / to / on / .
   ....
4 understand / clever / to / I'm / enough / Shakespeare / not / .
   ....
5 stage / high / was / climb / me / to / The / too / for / on / .
   ....
6 was / to / pass / I / not / enough / lucky / audition / the / .
   ....
7 painting / not / to / enough / good / win / prize / a / The / was / .
   ....
8 hard / to / seats / for / sit / were / The / on / too / us / .
   ....

3 Correct the mistakes in these sentences.

1 He was very nervous to go on the stage.
   He was too nervous to go on the stage.
2 It's too late for to get tickets for the gig.
   ....
3 The theatre is too far away that we can walk to.
   ....
4 Dad's guitar is too old to play it.
   ....
5 Is the ground dry enough to sit?
   ....
6 Our director thinks my voice is not enough good.
   ....
7 The near we get to the show, the scarier it all seems!
   ....
8 We had so a good time at the play!
   ....

4 Complete the second sentence so that it means the same as the first.

1 He couldn't wear the crown because it was so heavy.
   TOO
   The crown was _too heavy for him to_ wear.
2 As rock concerts become bigger, they get more exciting.
   THE
   ...., the more exciting they get.
3 He's too young to be a professional actor.
   ENOUGH
   He's .... a professional actor.
4 The performance was so good, I'm going to see it again.
   SUCH
   It was .... I'm going to see it again.
5 Are there any cheaper tickets for the show?
   THESE
   Are .... for the show?
6 Our music wasn't nearly as loud as yours.
   DEAL
   Your music was .... ours.
7 The final rehearsal was better than the first performance.
   AS
   The first performance .... the final rehearsal.
8 I'm not nearly as talented as my friend.
   FAR
   My friend .... me.

Grammar focus: articles

5 Complete the table by putting the nouns in the correct list.

> actor   album   ~~documentary~~
> growth   happiness   idea   love
> music   people   pride   programme
> success

Countable nouns		Uncountable nouns	
1	documentary	1	
2		2	
3		3	
4		4	
5		5	
6		6	

6 Complete the sentences with *a/an*, *the*, or -.

1 I really enjoyed ____the____ documentary about stage schools last night.

2 The producer was amazed at _____ success of the latest vampire movie.

3 I'm getting _____ car next year – Dad's promised me his old one!

4 The theme of the ballet is '_____ love in the time of war'.

5 The show was held to award _____ people who work behind the scenes in the theatre.

6 My all-time favourite single is *Money Can't Buy You* _____ *Happiness* by Jesse Jay.

7 _____ YouTube clip is a great way to show friends what you've been doing.

8 Alex was _____ homeless and busking on the streets when he was offered a recording contract.

9 I think _____ health is more important than fame.

10 Shakespeare's plays belong to _____ world, not to just one country.

7 Correct the mistakes in each of these sentences.

1 The health is an important concern for any actor.
Health is an important concern for any actor.

2 Without the love, the world would be a sad place.

3 I think my dad will have to buy the new car in a year or two.

4 French are excellent cooks.

5 Did you see a documentary they showed at 6 p.m. yesterday on the Discovery Channel?

6 You need the intelligence to be a great playwright like Shakespeare!

7 There's been huge growth in numbers of people using YouTube.

8 My brother's success has brought him the enormous happiness.

8 Complete the text by adding *a/an*, *the* or - in the gaps.

A Day in … Life of …. Dancer

Oliver Carter is 1) __*a*__ member of 2) _____ famous ballet company and is currently playing 3) _____ lead role as Romeo, in the ballet 'Romeo and Juliet'. Today, like 4) _____ most days in Oliver's life, is very busy. He starts with 5) _____ general practice classes; these follow 6) _____ same routine every day. After class, there's time for 7) _____ short break. Oliver and his friends find 8) _____ spare studio, put on 9) _____ music, and imagine they're dancing in 10) _____ club. They try out 11) _____ steps and tricks. If somebody has 12) _____ idea for a cool new step, 13) _____ others have a go at it, too. After 14) _____ break, it's back to serious business. First he has 15) _____ rehearsals to go to, then it's time for 16) _____ evening show. It's a busy life, but Oliver takes 17) _____ great pride in his dancing and is delighted with 18) _____ success he's had so far. For him, he says, 19) _____ life without dance would be unbearable.

Revision Unit 6

1 Choose the correct word.

1 Our youth club is planning to put *up/on/over* a concert.

2 What I enjoy most in my free time is listening to *music/the music/a music*.

3 A good friend should support you, not run you *up/out/down*.

4 Many people enjoy watching *the/–/a* good soap opera.

5 I'm sure there's no such thing as love *from/at/in* first sight.

6 I love *Italian/the Italian/an Italian* food.

7 She thinks she's in love but time will *say/speak/tell*!

8 That comedy film is *such/so/such a* funny!

9 Please hurry up and stop messing *around/up/on*!

10 *The/–/A* good friend is the most important thing you can have.

2 Complete the words in the sentences.

1 A d *i r e c t o* r is the person who is in charge of a play or film and tells actors what to do.

2 The events that form the main story of a play or film are called the p_____t.

3 An occasion when someone entertains people with a play or a piece of music is called a p____f_____c___.

4 A person in a book, play, film, etc is a ch_____c____r.

5 People who listen to or watch a performance are called the au_____ce.

6 A short performance by an actor to see if he or she is good enough for a part is called an au_____io___.

7 The clothes worn on stage by an actor are called a c___s_____e.

8 The time when all the people in a play practise before the performance is called a r___h_____s___l.

3 Complete the sentences with the correct form of the words in capitals.

1 Actors need to be ___*healthy*___ people. HEALTH

2 The _____ of getting up on stage and performing really scares me! THINK

3 We wanted to see the show but it was _____ to get tickets. POSSIBLE

4 My mum likes watching documentaries about _____ issues. SOCIETY

5 What is the _____ of the stage? WIDE

6 Are you coming to _____ club tonight? YOUNG

7 Sonya's got a _____ to make to you! CONFESS

8 I'm _____ going to be a rock singer one day soon! DEFINITE

4 Choose the correct answer, A, B or C.

1 The artist put a lot of _____ into his painting.
   A the love   **B** love   C a love

2 The members of the band are _____ nice people.
   A so   B such a   C such

3 We wish you lots of _____ in the future!
   A happiness
   B a happiness
   C the happiness

4 I think _____ should contribute more money to the arts.
   A rich   B the rich   C a rich

5 Pamela's off to _____ for three years to study drama.
   A university   B the university   C an university

6 Do you know who invented _____?
   A a car   B car   C the car

7 There was a good programme about _____ on TV last night.
   A the gorillas   B gorillas   C any gorillas

8 _____ advertisement on YouTube can bring in a lot of money, but this one didn't.
   A An   B Some   C The

5 Complete the text with one appropriate word in each space. Use any word once only.

◯◯◯ Confessions of a teen soap addict ⇦ ⇨ ⌂

My mum adores soap operas. If she didn't, I might never have become 1) _____ *as* _____ addicted as I am now. The more unlikely the storylines are, 2) _____ more she enjoys them. Personally, I like watching teen soaps far 3) _____ than adult ones, because they explore interesting teen problems, especially boy-girl relationships. You know the kind of chat that goes on: 'But prove that you love me more 4) _____ anything in the world!' or 'I've just met the 5) _____ gorgeous person in the world – but how do I get 6) _____ date?' Watching soaps is not just a waste of time, though – at least I don't think it is. I know a 7) _____ deal more about relationships now, for a start. And I'm a lot 8) _____ worried about dating new people – in fact, I'm quite relaxed about it now. But is that because I watch soaps or not? What do *you* think?

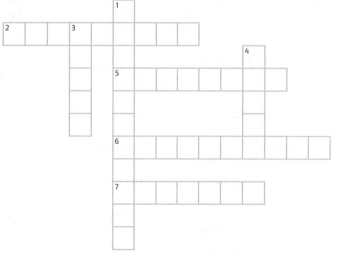

6 Rewrite the sentences using the words in capitals. Use between two and five words, including the word given.

1 There's no better musical in the theatre.
THE
This *is the best musical* in the theatre.

2 He spoke more slowly than anyone.
AS
Nobody spoke _____ .

3 The girls weren't as nervous as the boys.
LESS
The girls _____ the boys.

4 Each time I listen to that music I like it more.
I
The _____ that music, the more I like it.

5 How long is the stage?
THE
What _____ the stage?

6 I'm amazed at how strong he is.
HIS
I'm amazed _____ .

7 Complete the text with the best answer, A, B, C or D.

The Call of the Stage!

When I was just thirteen, my best friend 1) _____ me to compete in a talent show. I won, and it was 2) _____ best feeling in the world! Later, I joined a theatre group. They were busy 3) _____ on a musical – and I got the lead role. I was really nervous at the first 4) _____ . But the other actors were very friendly and I enjoyed 5) _____ out with them during breaks. I had to learn my lines off by 6) _____ of course – and my songs, too. On the opening night, I was scared – I thought everything might 7) _____ wrong. It didn't, thank goodness, and the play was 8) _____ success.

1	**A** challenged	**B**	bet	**C**	insisted	**D**	admitted
2	**A** a	**B**	some	**C**	just	**D**	the
3	**A** getting	**B**	putting	**C**	bringing	**D**	taking
4	**A** meetings	**B**	trials	**C**	rehearsals	**D**	practices
5	**A** hanging	**B**	sitting	**C**	relaxing	**D**	being
6	**A** memory	**B**	brain	**C**	heart	**D**	ear
7	**A** end	**B**	come	**C**	finish	**D**	go
8	**A** the	**B**	some	**C**	a	**D**	one

(1 A challenged is circled)

8 Use the clues to complete the crossword.

Across
2 To go to a party that you have not been invited to
5 To try very hard to achieve something difficult
6 An idiom that means to learn all of a piece of writing from memory
7 A phrasal verb that means 'criticise someone unkindly'

Down
1 A quick, intensive course
3 To leave home secretly to get married
4 To say somebody is responsible for something bad

07 school matters

VOCABULARY

1 Choose the correct words.

1 The boxer's *knuckles*/*ankles* were red because he'd been punching so hard.

2 My teacher is very *disciplined*/*strict* with us if we misbehave.

3 We're not allowed to run in any of the *corridors*/*alleys* in our school.

4 I had to stay after school for detention as a *correction*/*punishment* for missing class.

5 When Mum married Dad she kept her own *surname*/*nickname* instead of taking his.

6 If you want a teacher, you need to knock on the door of the *personnel*/*staff* room.

7 The class bully has been *expelled*/*excluded* for two weeks.

8 I prefer to learn at my own *grade*/*pace*.

2 Complete the sentences with these words.

> ~~forum~~   method   pace   punishment
> row   subject   torture   victim

1 Last night I gave my views in an online *forum* about modernising school buildings.

2 Mathematics used to be my worst _____ at school.

3 I think it's better if teachers let you learn at your own _____ .

4 I had to stay after school for detention as a _____ for missing class.

5 If you're a _____ of bullying, it's important that you tell an adult.

6 We sat in the back _____ of the cinema.

7 In my little sister's school, they've introduced a new _____ of teaching reading.

8 Studying for exams in summer is pure _____ .

3 Complete the words in the sentences.

1 I got into trouble at school so I was given de _t_ _e_ _n_ _t_ ion.

2 The classroom b_____y tried to order me around today.

3 We did a really interesting exp_____t in our science class today.

4 The new school t_____m starts on September 15th.

5 I'm going to have a private t_____r to help me with my maths.

6 My favourite s_____c_____s are English and history.

7 My parents put me in a bo_____d_____g school, so I only went home for the holidays.

8 If you want to be a school pr____f_____, you have to be a good leader.

9 Our teachers get angry if we don't p____r_____p_____ in class.

10 My real name is Pamela, but my n_____kn_____ is Poppy.

4 Complete the sentences with *make* or *do* in the correct form.

1 Oh no! I *have made* a huge mistake in my test and it's too late to correct it.

2 My mum says she just can't _____ without a dishwasher.

3 Don't _____ Paul laugh! He's trying to concentrate.

4 When Lucia hears that you've stolen her boyfriend, it'll _____ her cry.

5 _____ me a favour and lend me your phone, will you?

6 Tim _____ his best in the test today, but he doesn't think he's passed.

7 I'm hopeless at _____ decisions!

8 We _____ an experiment in class and the test tube exploded!

5 Choose the correct answer, A, B, C or D.

1 I was shocked at the .... remarks the bully made.
- **A** vicious
- **B** hard
- **C** violent
- **D** tough

2 The boys who painted graffiti on the school walls are complete ....
- **A** gangs
- **B** bullies
- **C** torturers
- **D** vandals

3 Our teacher encouraged us all to .... in the drama class.
- **A** include
- **B** participate
- **C** take
- **D** enjoy

4 I think they should .... school uniforms all round the world.
- **A** abolish
- **B** exclude
- **C** expel
- **D** abandon

5 You'll get punished if you disobey the school ....
- **A** laws
- **B** rules
- **C** orders
- **D** rulers

6 What .... did you get in your exam?
- **A** notes
- **B** remarks
- **C** numbers
- **D** grades

6 Complete the sentences with these words.

> detect   distance learning   hand
> ~~online~~   rules   state of the art
> step   take

1 Part of our coursework involves doing ......*online*...... research.

2 Next year I have to .... exams to get into medical school.

3 Examiners can .... cheats by checking on exam candidates' handwriting.

4 We're not allowed to type the essay – we've got to write it out by ....

5 They threw him out of the gang because he wouldn't follow their ....

6 You've helped me a lot, but could you go one .... further and type this out for me?

7 We've got a brand new, ... gym in our school.

8 If you live too far from a university to go there regularly, you can study by .... instead.

7 Choose the correct answer.

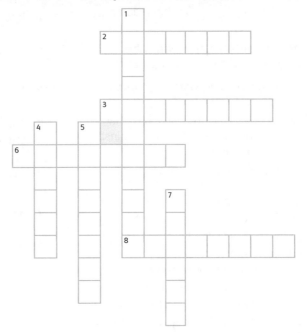

View previous comments   Cancel Share Post

I've been participating in an 1) *outline*/*online* forum about examinations. We've been discussing whether we'd prefer to 2) *take*/*make* one big, end-of-year exam, or be tested regularly during each school 3) *period*/*term*. I don't get stressed by exams and I usually get good 4) *notes*/*grades*, so exams aren't a problem for me. But I know other students who consider them 5) *torture*/*injury* and would be really happy if exams were 6) *excluded*/*abolished* for good. The problem with continuous tests or assessment is that it's not difficult for students to 7) *fault*/*cheat*. If this coursework is written out by hand, examiners can easily 8) *tell*/*detect* cheating. But these days most students type their coursework. So are final exams fairer? What do *you* think?

Write a comment   Support

8 Use the clues to complete the crossword.

Across
2 People who deliberately damage things
3 A short or friendly name given to you by friends and family
6 To completely destroy a building
8 To be forbidden to come to school for a period of time

Down
1 A verb meaning *take part in*
4 A verb meaning *to notice something that is not easy to see*
5 A long passageway in a school
7 Someone who has been attacked

GRAMMAR
Grammar focus: the passive

1 Complete the sentences with the missing word.

1 Has your mobile phone _____been_____ found yet?
2 You won't _____ allowed to wear that to school!
3 It's not fair! Our teachers _____ us do so much homework!
4 My sister's not _____ to have a tattoo. My parents have forbidden it.
5 I _____ never been punished for cheating.
6 The best students _____ given prizes in the ceremony yesterday.
7 I hope I _____ not be asked to read my essay out loud in class tomorrow.
8 By the time I got to the school party, all the cakes _____ been eaten!

2 Complete the sentences with the correct form of the verb in brackets.

1 The exam results _were announced_ (announce) yesterday.
2 We _____ (not/allow) to take mobile phones into class. It's against the school rules.
3 As this very moment my brother _____ for a place at university. (interview)
4 In our school, cheating _____ (punish) very severely.
5 Our new sports block _____ (open) by a celebrity next week.
6 We had to study in the café while our classroom _____. (redecorate)
7 By the time the fire engine arrived, the fire in the science lab _____. (put out)
8 _____ of the date of the trip by the school yet? (you/inform)

3 Complete the second sentence so that it means the same as the first.

1 They gave the student a warning about her behaviour.
The student _was given a warning about her behaviour_.
2 They are demolishing the old gymnasium.
The old gymnasium _____.
3 They don't let students leave the school at lunchtime.
Students _____.
4 Has anyone told the teacher what happened?
Has the _____?
5 Someone is telling my friend off at this minute.
My friend _____.
6 They made us all stay in school for detention.
We _____.
7 Is anyone taking care of the visitors?
Are _____?
8 They will appoint a new member of staff next term.
A new member of staff _____.

4 Put the words in the correct order.

1 students / made / write / to / the / were / lines / .
The students were made to write lines.
2 been / not / the / Has / cleaned / yet / classroom?
_____
3 flowers / given / teacher / was / The / .
_____
4 How / cook / taught / to / were / you / ?
_____
5 spend / was / Each / ten dollars / spend / given / to / student / .
_____
6 been / repaired / yet / computer / the / Has / ?
_____
7 allowed / to / We / jeans / not / are / wear / school / in / .
_____
8 post / results / Will / sent / in / our / be / exam / the / ?
_____

Grammar focus: more passive forms

5 Rewrite the sentences using the words in capitals. Use between two and five words, including the word given.

1 They were always punishing James.
GETTING
James was always getting punished.

2 They forced me to have extra violin lessons.
MADE
I _____ extra violin lessons .

3 Teachers were planning the new timetable.
PLANNED
The new timetable _____ teachers.

4 They won't let us study outdoors.
ALLOWED
We _____ outdoors.

5 That printer needs repairing.
SHOULD
That printer _____ .

6 Are they still making CDs these days?
MADE
Are CDs _____ these days?

6 Choose the correct answer, A, B or C.

1 Our classroom needs to _____ .
   A redecorate
   B being redecorated
   C be redecorated

2 Do you agree that uniforms _____ ?
   A they should be banned
   B should ban
   C should be banned

3 My sister _____ me to help her with her homework.
   A got
   B had
   C made

4 Cheats ought _____ .
   A to punish
   B to be punished
   C to be punishing

5 The playground should _____ by now.
   A it be reopened
   B being reopened
   C be reopened

6 That printer needs _____ .
   A to repair
   B repairing
   C to have repaired

7 Complete the sentences with *have*, *get* or *need* in an appropriate form and a verb from the box.

clean   ~~have cut~~   take out   wash

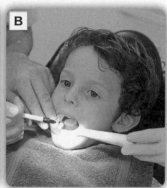

1 My sister *is having* her hair *cut* today.

2 Tom _____ a tooth _____ yesterday.

3 My dad _____ me _____ his car.

4 Those windows _____ !

8 Complete the sentences with an appropriate form of the verb in brackets.

1 Dad's got to *get the car serviced* .
(get/the car/service)

2 _____ like I asked you?
(get/those notes/type)

3 Oh no! I _____ . (have/my phone/steal)

4 There's something wrong with your bicycle. It _____ . (need/check)

5 You can _____ if you're brave enough.
(get/yourself/tattoo)

6 I wear glasses and I need to _____ every two years. (have/my eyes/test)

7 Did you make this mess? _____ now!
(Get/it/tidy)

8 Excuse me! Can I _____ here?
(get/my photos/enlarge)

Revision Unit 7

1 Choose the correct answer, A, B, C or D.

1 The content of that bully's email was really _____ .
   (A) vicious B strict C violent D passive

2 Love is the main _____ of the book I'm reading.
   A area B theme C part D plot

3 Who was _____ for breaking the glass?
   A guilty B blaming
   C responsible D embarrassed

4 Football _____ covered the walls in graffiti.
   A gangs B bullies C victims D vandals

5 Before I write my essay, I need to do a lot of _____ into the subject.
   A research B study
   C study D searching

6 I really like the first _____ of that story.
   A row B line C speech D subject

7 Why don't you type that instead of writing it all out _____ hand?
   A by B from C with D in

8 The teacher wasn't _____ that Sally was cheating.
   A awake B known C alert D aware

2 Complete the sentences with these words.

> detect exclude grade ~~pace~~
> participate row strict term

1 I don't want to hurry this; I'd prefer to work at a steady _pace_ .

2 Examiners are always trying to _____ if we're cheating.

3 They're planning to _____ Emma for bullying another girl.

4 The drama teacher makes us _____ in all the activities.

5 What _____ did you get in the exam?

6 If we hurry, we can sit in the back _____ of the lecture room.

7 I wish the head teacher wasn't always so _____ .

8 I can't believe it's the last day of _____ tomorrow!

3 Read the blog and choose the best answer, A, B, C or D.

> View previous comments   Cancel   Share   Post
>
> If I were a teacher for just one day, I'd cut the length of the school 1) _____ so that students had longer holidays. I'd rewrite all those boring school 2) _____ about what students can and cannot do – like text friends in class. Next, I'd get the 3) _____ changed so that the most boring 4) _____ are dropped for good. I wouldn't be a pushover, but I wouldn't be too 5) _____ , either. Of course, I wouldn't 6) _____ my students wear a uniform. I'd 7) _____ them dress exactly how they like. Oh, and I'd 8) _____ single-sex schools, too. So, would I make a good teacher? What do *you* think?
>
> Write a comment   Support

1 A day   B period   C row   (D) term
2 A rules   B laws   C orders   D lines
3 A diary   B calendar C timetable D routine
4 A themes   B subjects C topics   D areas
5 A strict   B rough   C laid-back D patient
6 A force   B control C require   D make
7 A free   B enable   C let   D allow
8 A expel   B abolish C punish   D exclude

4 Find ten words on the topic of schools and education. The words go across, down or diagonally. The first letter of each word is highlighted.

a	t	h	o	m	e	w	o	r	k	d	b	o
x	h	j	q	a	d	w	z	e	t	e	d	z
c	o	r	r	i	d	o	r	j	y	t	s	x
c	e	s	e	e	p	n	y	x	h	e	g	s
l	u	s	e	n	x	r	t	l	p	n	l	y
a	s	u	x	n	h	c	e	a	v	t	i	g
s	t	b	p	u	a	f	l	n	d	i	o	r
s	r	j	e	u	a	p	d	u	t	o	e	a
r	i	e	l	w	b	b	q	z	d	n	f	d
o	c	c	l	a	m	h	j	y	i	e	c	e
o	t	t	e	s	y	j	t	k	z	b	d	s
m	s	s	d	i	s	c	i	p	l	i	n	e

5 Rewrite the sentences in the passive. Use by + agent only where necessary.

1 Someone taught me to type when I was very young.
I was taught to type when I was very young.

2 A nurse has just given us a talk on smoking.

3 Is someone going to announce the date of the next concert soon?

4 The headteacher is telling the students the result of their exams.

5 They never let students go into the staffroom.

6 The government paid the headteacher thousands of dollars.

7 Did someone give you that bicycle for your birthday?

8 A policeman made me cross the road on a proper crossing.

6 Rewrite these sentences correctly.

1 This work must to be rewritten!
This work must be rewritten!

2 Your desk needs to be fixing.

3 We've had installed new computers in our school library.

4 Last week, I got my brother do my homework for me!

5 Has anything been doing to solve your problem yet?

6 In my opinion, holidays they should definitely be longer!

7 My hair needs to cut.

8 I wasn't let to go to the club last weekend.

7 Complete the blog with one word in each space.

View previous comments   Cancel   Share   Post

If I 1) ___*were*___ asked what 2) _____ be done to improve my school, I'd have a lot of suggestions. The biggest thing that 3) _____ changing is the timetable. We 4) _____ taught a huge variety of subjects, but I want to study subjects that I find exciting. I think the timetable ought to 5) _____ planned much more around individuals and their interests. Another thing that needs 6) _____ be changed is the rule about uniforms. At my sister's school they are 7) _____ to wear what they like, but at my school we are 8) _____ to wear this awful uniform, even in senior classes. It's ridiculous!

Write a comment   Support

8 Rewrite the sentences using the words in capitals. Use between two and five words, including the word given.

1 Mum's getting someone to paint her nails for her.
PAINTED
Mum's *getting/having her nails painted* .

2 Someone ought to fix that broken window.
NEEDS
That window _____ .

3 That work was supposed to be done by now.
SHOULD
That work _____ by now.

4 Nobody let us miss lessons.
WERE
We _____ lessons.

5 They're going to offer our teacher promotion.
IS
Our teacher _____ promotion.

6 I got someone to update my laptop.
HAD
I _____ .

7 They really must change the timetable.
BE
The timetable really _____ .

8 Dad made me wash the dishes last night.
GOT
Dad _____ last night.

Technology rules!

VOCABULARY

1 Label the items in the pictures.

> computer   games console
> keyboard   mouse   screen

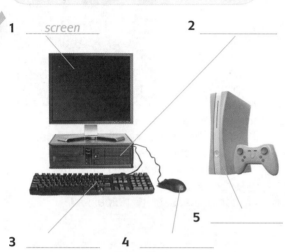

1 _screen_
2 ....
3 ....
4 ....
5 ....

2 Complete the sentences with these words in the correct form.

> access   boast   ~~edit~~   flirt
> gossip   misinterpret   swap
> tease

1 I've typed my story so now I need to _edit_ it and send off for the competition.
2 Can I .... pens with you for a minute? I can write much better with that one.
3 If you're going to .... about me, you could at least get your facts right!
4 Ben is always .... about how clever he is. He makes me sick!
5 Jessica .... what I said and now she won't speak to me at all.
6 My friends are always .... me because I have really thin legs.
7 Go to an Internet café and you can .... the Internet and have a coffee, too!
8 My brother and my best friend are so keen on each other it's embarrassing – they're always .... in the corridor.

3 Choose the correct answer, A, B, C or D.

1 My friends and I joined an online .... room to discuss our problem.
   (A) chat   **B** gossip   **C** talk   **D** discuss
2 There weren't enough books so we had to ....
   A buy   **B** lend   **C** share   **D** borrow
3 I've just .... a blog on the Internet.
   A sent   **B** messaged   **C** made   **D** posted
4 When Peter looks at Facebook, he'll see that I've left a 'Happy Birthday' message on his ....
   A clip   **B** wall   **C** modem   **D** screen
5 Look on YouTube and you'll see a .... of Ben and I at last night's gig.
   A hit   **B** film   **C** clip   **D** snap
6 Please don't order me about in class. I'm not your .... !
   A slave   **B** waiter   **C** prey   **D** victim
7 Do you know who first .... the Internet?
   A discovered   **B** found   **C** manufactured   **D** invented
8 Don't worry if you can't print out your essay – we'll .... the problem somehow!
   A get about   **B** get off   **C** get round   **D** get into

4 Find ten words on the topic of technology. The words go across, down or diagonally. The first letter of each word is highlighted.

v	l	m	e	f	r	o	u	t	e	r	e	y	v	c
y	p	v	e	k	b	g	t	q	l	f	g	l	t	a
j	s	y	m	o	m	l	k	b	l	b	e	c	w	w
h	d	i	a	o	y	p	o	c	s	c	r	e	e	n
c	f	p	t	z	u	o	s	r	a	x	r	i	z	n
g	u	n	v	e	p	s	o	n	l	i	n	e	q	z
h	a	n	a	d	u	a	e	c	l	o	x	l	n	n
g	k	d	g	i	a	s	t	r	o	n	o	m	y	o
c	e	c	g	r	d	i	h	r	d	n	t	l	y	r
u	y	i	i	e	b	i	v	p	i	g	s	s	k	s
g	b	h	x	c	t	p	q	t	g	e	u	o	y	v
s	o	v	x	t	s	j	j	i	x	a	p	l	b
a	a	z	o	o	h	j	m	e	t	y	o	z	v	e
w	r	g	b	r	o	a	d	b	a	n	d	z	f	c
o	d	e	u	a	k	x	r	y	l	b	l	g	n	o

5 Complete the table.

	Verb	Noun	Adjective
1	civilise	civilisation	civilised
2	involve		xxxxxx
3	xxxxxx	democracy	
4	pollute		
5	achieve		achievable
6	observe		observable
7	xxxxxx	obstinacy	
8	encourage		encouraging

6 Complete the sentences with the correct form of the word in capitals.

1 As a teenager, I value my _independence_ .
INDEPENDENT

2 Getting a first class Honours degree would be a great _____.
ACHIEVE

3 Sarah made a really clever _____ in class today.
OBSERVE

4 I had no _____ in arranging the tennis competition at all, so don't blame me!
INVOLVE

5 My best friend is really _____ and won't change her mind once she's made it up.
OBSTINACY

6 We've been studying the Mayan _____ in our history classes.
CIVILISE

7 Our teachers are great because they give us so much _____.
ENCOURAGE

8 Do you know how many countries in the world have _____ governments?
DEMOCRACY

7 Complete the article with the correct form of the words in capitals.

8 Use the clues to complete the crossword.

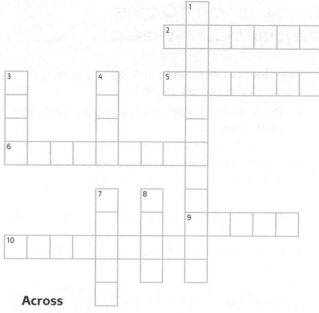

Across

2 The organs in your body that clean your blood.

5 If you have a _____ camera, you can review and delete your photos.

6 The noun you can form from *know*.

9 To *get* _____ *something* is a phrasal verb which means *to overcome a problem*.

10 The adjective you can form from *obstinacy*.

Down

1 To understand something wrongly

3 To _____ *something* up is a phrasal verb which means *to support or confirm something*.

4 The place where friends write messages to you on Facebook.

7 To behave towards someone in a way that shows you may be attracted to them

8 To give something to someone in exchange for something else

The Greatest Invention?

Among the great 1) _achievements_ of all time, which would you put top? Past 2) _____ might have chosen sending a man into space. But for me, the greatest achievement of all time is the invention of the Internet. Now we can access information and increase our general 3) _____ with one click of a key. Now we can meet friends at any time of day on 4) _____ networking sites, or make video clips with friends and upload them for all the world to see. Networking sites can have disadvantages, though. Some parents feel their child's 5) _____ is being invaded, or that the wrong people may be able to view their personal details. But in spite of these 6) _____, sites like Facebook are 7) _____ popular. A word of warning though! Teachers and future employers may see what you put on the net. Post photos of yourself behaving badly and you'll leave them with a poor 8) _____ of your character!

ACHIEVE
CIVILISE

KNOW
SOCIETY

PRIVATE

OBJECT
EXTREME

IMPRESS

GRAMMAR
Grammar focus: reported speech

1 Complete the reported questions by putting the words in the correct order.

1 The head teacher wanted to know / we / done / what / had / .
The head teacher wanted to know what we had done.

2 The shop assistant asked / us / help / could / if / he / .

3 My dad wanted to know / where / I / been / had / .

4 My friend wondered / free / go / was / if / to / out / I / .

5 Marie asked / whether / was / gig / going / Jamie / the / to / .

6 We wanted to know / working / why / not / was / computer / the / .

7 I asked / knew / singer / of / the / Tracy / asked / she / name / the / if / .

8 John asked / seen / clip / I / if / his / YouTube / had / on / .

2 Finish putting the direct speech quotes into reported speech.

1 Someone wrote a nice comment on Linda's wall.
I was told that *someone had written a nice comment on Linda's wall* .

2 I'm starting a new school next term.
The boy next door said _____ .

3 What time are you going out?
Dad wanted to know _____ .

4 Did you remember to buy your aunt a birthday card?
Mum wanted to know _____ .

5 We're going to book a holiday in France, so you can practise your French.
My parents announced that _____ .

6 Have you found the money you lost?
My friend wondered _____ .

7 Adam's just gone to get his book.
I told the teacher _____ .

8 I dropped Adele's ring and now we can't find it.
I explained to Peter that _____ .

3 Read this conversation between George and his grandad. Then put it into reported speech, making all necessary changes.

Grandad: 1) Can you help with something, George?
George: 2) What's the problem, Grandad?
Grandad: 3) I'm having trouble with my laptop. I can't get my emails.
George: 4) Are you sure you've got an Internet connection?
Grandad: 5) I'm not sure, but it was working OK yesterday.
George: 6) I'll just check. There may be a problem with our telephone line.
Grandad: 7) Oh, does that affect the Internet?
George: 8) Yes it does, Grandad! But don't worry, I'll get your laptop working again soon.

1 *Grandad asked me if I could help him with something.*
2 _____
3 _____
4 _____
5 _____
6 _____
7 _____
8 _____

4 Complete the text with one word in each space.

Hacking – Is it a Crime?

I was doing a project on hacking, so I asked the teacher 1) *if/whether* he knew the name of the most famous hacker in the world. He 2) _____ me it was a man called Kevin Mitnik. Mitnik spent five years in jail for breaking into the computer systems of some major companies. But he claimed 3) _____ wasn't guilty of many of these crimes. He complained that the media 4) _____ misrepresented him. He admitted that he 5) _____ a hacker, but said that, for him, hacking was not something bad. When journalists asked him 6) _____ he believed that, he told 7) _____ that hacking used to be respected as a skill.
He 8) _____ he'd never tried to steal credit card information or to rob anyone. But is hacking really a respectable activity? What do *you* think ?

Grammar focus: reporting verbs

5 Complete the sentences with these verbs in their correct form. Use each verb once only.

> admit   invite   order   persuade
> remind   suggest   thank   ~~warn~~

1 My friends _warned_ me that making friends with the class bully was a big mistake.
2 Thank goodness you _____ me to take my phone with me; I couldn't have got help without it.
3 Wendy _____ meeting in the Internet café. Is that OK with you?
4 I didn't want to go to the pool, but in the end my little brother _____ me to take him there.
5 The policeman _____ the gang members to empty their pockets.
6 Darren _____ to me that he had dropped the MP3 player and broken it.
7 Has Bob _____ you to go to the cinema with him? He's shy about asking you!
8 We _____ our neighbours for looking after the cat and gave them a gift.

6 Complete the sentences in reported speech.

1 I'm sorry I hurt your feelings.
  Kylie apologised _for hurting my feelings_ .
2 I'm so tired!
  Robert complained _____ .
3 I wish I hadn't bought this make of camera.
  She regretted _____ .
4 Go on! Make a clip for YouTube, Paul!
  I encouraged Paul _____ .
5 Let's go out.
  My friend suggested _____ .
6 Would you like to come to my party, James?
  I invited _____ .
7 Sit down and be quiet!
  The teacher ordered me _____ .
8 It's true – I did borrow your phone without asking you.
  Paul admitted _____ .

7 Identify the six sentences which contain one unnecessary word and correct them.

1 The company is believed to have it brought out a new version of their software.
2 The engineer he is thought to have repaired the fault.
3 The gang are not believed to have been stolen all the computers.
4 Hackers are said to have discovered some secret information.
5 It is said that technology will it have changed the world beyond recognition in 100 years' time.
6 Tablet computers are reported to be now being in use in most classrooms in this area.
7 It is claimed that the new make of tablet computer has some major faults.
8 The new brand of smart phone is thought to have been outsold all other brands.

8 Complete the second sentence so that it means the same as the first.

1 People say that robots may take over the world one day.
  SAID
  It _is said that_ robots may take over the world one day.
2 They believe that hackers have got past their computer security system.
  BELIEVED
  Hackers _____ past the police security system.
3 They report a new social network site is gaining popularity.
  REPORTED
  A new social network site _____ popularity.
4 People say we are too dependent on technology.
  ARE
  We _____ too dependent on technology.
5 They claim that the new software is the best on the market.
  TO
  The new software _____ the best on the market.
6 They say that a child created the latest best-selling phone app.
  IS
  A child _____ the latest best-selling phone app.
7 It is believed that the fire started due to a fault in a computer.
  HAVE
  The fire _____ due to a fault in a computer.

Revision Unit 8

1 Choose the correct word, A, B or C.

1 I know you came top in the test. There's no need to _____ .
  A gossip **(B)** boast **C** tease

2 You saw what happened, so will you _____ my story?
  A put up **B** stand up **C** back up

3 Chris and I always _____ CDs with each other after we've finished with them.
  A swap **B** sort **C** share

4 Did you know that a man called Douglas Engelbart _____ the computer mouse?
  A discovered **B** did **C** invented

5 Pamela's dad is always buying the latest _____ , like new smartphones and tablet computers.
  A appliances **B** gadgets **C** machines

6 At the weekend, I'm going to _____ with some of my best mates.
  A hang up **B** hang together **C** hang out

7 I need to _____ this music from iTunes onto my MP3 player.
  A download **B** edit **C** access

8 My YouTube clip is really popular – it's getting lots of _____ .
  A prints **B** hits **C** punches

2 Complete the sentences with words from the box.

~~broadband~~ digital mouse online
screen site user viral

1 How much do you pay per month for _broadband_ and who's your provider?

2 Tanya's YouTube clip has gone _____ ; she's had thousands of hits.

3 Which _____ should I go on to get information for my coursework?

4 To go _____ , you need to be connected to the Internet.

5 The battery has gone flat in my _____ , so now I can't move the cursor or type anything.

6 My brother is a big _____ of Facebook. He's on it all the time!

7 You'll need to clean the _____ of that computer. It's so dusty you can't read a word on it.

8 The _____ revolution is changing our world very quickly.

3 Form nouns from the words below.

1 social → _society_
2 independent →
3 private →
4 know →
5 involve →
6 imagine →
7 assess →
8 evident →

4 Complete the words in the sentences.

1 The d _i_ _g_ i _t_ _a_ l revolution has brought us mobile phones and tablets.

2 Teenagers are big users of social n___ w_____ sites.

3 We must change our bro_____ provider; this one is too expensive.

4 We made the bully c_____e_____ to the cruel things he'd done.

5 How many letters are there on a computer k___y_____ d. Do you know?

6 I felt really p_____ck_____ the first time I took an IT exam.

7 You should be careful what you write in an email in case people mis_____t_____ it.

8 I don't want to be a s_____e to technology.

5 Identify the six sentences which contain one unnecessary word and correct them.

1 Freya wanted to know where did I got my smartphone from.

2 Mum told to my sister to stop using Facebook.

3 Toby wanted to know whether Clare she was coming to the party.

4 A friend asked me if I knew the French teacher's address.

5 My classmates insisted on they were right.

6 The technician suggested I turning the computer off and then on again.

7 Dad reminded me to look up the information.

8 The teacher explained us that he had been ill the previous day.

6 **Choose the correct answer, A, B or C.**

1 I asked my friend how long _____ .
  A she had been waiting
  B had she been waiting
  C had been she waiting

2 The policeman ordered Gloria _____ .
  A going to the police station
  B go to the police station
  C to go to the police station

3 Tom suggested _____ our own video clip.
  A making
  B us to make
  C us making

4 My sister apologised _____ at me.
  A for shouting
  B to shout
  C that she shouted

5 We encouraged Sue _____ her old phone.
  A into selling
  B to sell
  C that she sell

6 Vandals _____ broken into the computer room.
  A they said to have
  B they are said to have
  C are said to have

7 It _____ computer chips will become much smaller in the future.
  A is believed that
  B believed that
  C is believing that

8 A scientist is reported _____ a car that drives itself.
  A he has invented
  B to have invented
  C having invented

7 **Complete the sentences with one word in each space.**

8 **Complete the second sentence so that it means the same as the first.**

1 'I'll buy your old laptop, Jenny.'
  OFFERED
  Harry _offered to buy_ Jenny's old laptop.

2 'Shall we text the rest of the group?', Dan said.
  SUGGESTED
  Dan _____ the rest of the group.

3 They say that YouTube gets thousands of hits a day.
  SAID
  YouTube _____ thousands of hits a day.

4 'Did Berners Lee invent the Internet?'
  WHETHER
  My friend wanted to know _____ the Internet.

5 'We're sorry we didn't phone you yesterday, Amy.'
  APOLOGISED
  Amy's friends _____ .

6 They think children are coping well with the digital world.
  THOUGHT
  Children _____ well with the digital world.

7 'Turn off the television immediately', my dad said.
  ORDERED
  My dad _____ the television.

8 It was impossible to stop Craig from playing on the computer.
  INSISTED
  Craig _____ on the computer.

Have you ever used your parents' credit card to buy 1) _something_ online? If you have, I'm sure your parents warned you 2) _____ take great care – and they were right to do so! Thieves 3) _____ believed to be making thousands of dollars from online fraud. My family were victims of this kind of fraud last month. My parents are very nervous of online shopping, but I persuaded 4) _____ to let me buy a pair of jeans from a new website. My friend advised me 5) _____ to use the site because it might not be safe, but I took no notice. A few days later, my mum got a call from the credit card company. They told her that $4,000 6) _____ been taken from our card in one go by fraudsters! Of course, I apologised to my parents 7) _____ being so stupid, but they were really angry. I really regret 8) _____ so careless – and I won't do any online shopping again for a long time!

VOCABULARY

1 Decide if the adjectives describe good or bad qualities and put them in the correct list.

> cruel   disrespectful   easy-going
> fussy   generous   polite   rebellious
> stubborn   tolerant   unselfish
> well-behaved

Good qualities	Bad qualities
well-behaved	

2 Complete the sentences with the correct form of the word in capitals.

1 Tom's _rebellion_ against the school rules led to him him being expelled.
REBEL

2 My sister got a prize for good _____ .
BEHAVE

3 Our uncle died last year so my aunt is now _____ .
WIDOW

4 Paul is really kind and _____ .
HELP

5 Dad's pleased because my school report says there's been a great _____ in my attitude to school!
IMPROVE

6 Laura got on much better in class after the _____ of the new teacher.
ARRIVE

7 I can't believe you were so _____ to your gran. You were really rude!
RESPECT

8 My little brother is terribly _____ and is always getting told off.
OBEDIENT

3 Complete the sentences with these words.

> giggle   hit   nightmare   open   rude   ~~sight~~

1 When my mum met my dad, it was love at first _sight_ !

2 My penfriend came to stay last week and we didn't get on; in fact, she was a total _____ !

3 Fran gets on well with her teacher, so perhaps she'll _____ up to him about the problem.

4 Mum _____ the roof when she saw my tattoo!

5 I got a _____ awakening when I came bottom of the class this year!

6 My friend and I wore awful, coloured wigs to the party just for a _____ .

4 Choose the correct word, A, B or C.

1 I'm sorry, but I don't want to _____ with you about this any more.
A dispute   B argue   C dialogue

2 I really _____ having to wash the dishes every evening.
A object   B resent   C refuse

3 If Grace is rude to you, just try and _____ it.
A neglect   B reject   C ignore

4 I hate having _____ with my family, but they never last long.
A lines   B rows   C bans

5 My parents only give me pocket money if I help with the household _____ .
A jobs   B works   C chores

6 Dad's _____ me from going to the youth club for a month.
A forbidden   B banned   C ordered

5 Choose the correct word.

1 We *felt/took* sorry for the new girl and let her join our gang.

2 My brother is so spoiled that he shouts and screams if he can't *get/go* his own way.

3 Maria stole my boyfriend, but I'll *get/make* my own back one day!

4 I've *done/made* friends with the boy next door.

5 The bully soon *backed/stood* down when the teacher came into the room.

6 Ryan got left *down/out* of the football team for the match on Friday and he's so disappointed.

7 I'm sorry if I upset you; please don't let us *fall/walk* out.

8 Pay no attention to George; he's just trying to *do/make* trouble.

6 Complete the sentences with these words.

arrest   burgle   charge
~~interview~~   judge   mug
probation   victim

1 The police decided to take the man back to the police station and ___*interview*___ him.

2 Always lock your door when you go out in case somebody tries to break in and _____ your house.

3 Don't make it obvious you're carrying so much cash, or somebody might _____ you.

4 For one year after leaving jail, the woman had to report to her _____ officer every month.

5 If you drink and drive, the police may stop you, _____ you and take you to a police station.

6 The _____ sent the murderer to jail for life.

7 The police took the man to the police station, but they couldn't _____ him because they didn't have enough evidence.

8 The _____ of the robbery was shocked but not injured, thank goodness.

7 Complete the article with the best answer, A, B, C or D.

Subject: **My new house!**

My brother William had a 1) _____ awakening last week. He'd recently 2) _____ friends with a gang of teenagers who my parents really didn't like. The gang were always 3) _____ trouble in our neighbourhood, especially when they 4) _____ out with other teenage gangs. Anyway, last week my brother thought a neighbour was making 5) _____ of his new haircut, so he started a fight. A police car arrived soon afterwards, and the officer said he was going to 6) _____ William. William was defiant at first, but he 7) _____ down when a police dog jumped out of the car! He then realised he was in big trouble and stared crying! Luckily for William, his victim was kind-hearted and felt 8) _____ for him. He asked the policeman to let William off with a warning. I don't think my brother will be hanging out with a gang again for a long time!

1	**A** rude	**B** sad	**C** rough	**D** large
2	**A** done	**B** been	**C** made	**D** formed
3	**A** doing	**B** making	**C** being	**D** getting
4	**A** fell	**B** went	**C** fought	**D** did
5	**A** laugh	**B** fun	**C** enjoyment	**D** silly
6	**A** suspend	**B** charge	**C** arrest	**D** exclude
7	**A** jumped	**B** went	**C** stood	**D** backed
8	**A** sad	**B** pity	**C** unhappy	**D** sorry

8 Find ten words in the wordsearch on the topic of personality and behaviour. The words go across, down or diagonally. The first letter of each word is highlighted.

e	w	f	o	a	q	n	n	f	l	f	j	i	w	n
q	s	r	s	g	j	a	l	s	r	a	c	h	e	d
j	j	k	f	e	c	s	p	v	u	c	h	z	o	d
m	w	y	m	n	r	t	m	t	g	q	a	u	c	i
i	c	e	m	e	b	y	e	o	a	b	r	q	n	y
q	z	a	c	r	x	g	n	b	u	c	m	h	p	m
b	x	s	f	o	v	w	v	n	r	l	i	r	c	s
m	q	y	l	u	i	v	i	o	a	o	n	d	s	p
w	c	g	e	s	h	g	r	x	l	a	g	n	p	i
z	l	o	x	w	s	m	o	i	d	r	b	x	o	t
p	f	i	i	h	h	o	n	o	p	f	m	z	i	e
l	e	n	b	y	y	o	m	u	v	p	d	w	l	f
z	b	g	l	s	b	d	e	s	o	f	s	c	e	u
r	p	f	e	b	j	y	n	e	f	s	l	c	d	l
f	u	w	a	j	o	u	t	r	a	g	e	o	u	s

GRAMMAR
Grammar focus: modal verbs

1 **Choose the correct answer, A, B or C.**

1 Duncan _____ speak French really well.
  - **A** ought
  - **B** is able
  - **C** can ✓

2 You _____ shout at me – I'm not doing anything wrong.
  - **A** needn't
  - **B** can't
  - **C** don't need

3 Why _____ argue with Peter? He's really upset now.
  - **A** did you ought to
  - **B** could you
  - **C** did you have to

4 You _____ try to buy alcohol if you're under the legal age to do so.
  - **A** mustn't
  - **B** couldn't
  - **C** don't need to

5 I'm sure Emma _____ be out alone so late at night – do her parents know where she is?
  - **A** can't
  - **B** shouldn't
  - **C** doesn't need

6 I'm really annoyed that I _____ to go to the music festival last weekend.
  - **A** wasn't let
  - **B** couldn't
  - **C** wasn't allowed

2 **Complete the sentences with modal verbs in the positive or negative form. There may be more than one correct answer.**

1 I know I _must_ not use bad language so don't worry, I'll be careful.

2 Why did you _____ go to bed so early last night? What had you done wrong?

3 How _____ you speak to your mum like that? Apologise at once!

4 Hurray! It's a holiday tomorrow so I _____ to get up early.

5 I _____ text you yesterday because my dad has taken my phone off me!

6 If I were you, I _____ see a doctor about your cough.

3 **Complete the text with one word in each space.**

> 💬 View previous comments   Cancel Share Post
>
> **How to deal with bullies**
> There are lots of bullies around. You 1) ___can___ find them at school, and at work, too. Mike was our school bully. He was a big guy and he scared the younger kids so much they felt they 2) _____ to do everything he told them. They were never 3) _____ to disagree – they didn't dare, because they knew Mike 4) _____ make their lives very difficult if he wanted – by putting cruel remarks on Facebook, for example, or telling lies about them. So, why was Mike a bully? Well, like all bullies he had personal problems that he could 5) _____ – or would not – discuss. Because he had no confidence in himself, he felt he 6) _____ to make his victims feel insecure, too. Luckily, Mikes' victims soon realised that they didn't have 7) _____ put up with his behaviour. Their friends had already advised them that they 8) _____ tell the headteacher. They did, and Mike soon found himself in the headteacher's office. There was no more bullying at our school for a very long time after that.
>
> Write a comment   Support

4 **Rewrite the sentences using the words in capitals. Use between two and five words, including the word given.**

1 You don't have to come if you don't want to.
  NEED
  You _needn't/don't need to come_ if you don't want to.

2 My advice is to talk to your parents about it.
  OUGHT
  I think you _____ to your parents about it.

3 Our parents didn't let us stay out late last night.
  ALLOWED
  We _____ out late last night.

4 We were obliged to help with the housework.
  TO
  We _____ with the housework.

5 I'm sorry I couldn't go on the trip with you.
  ABLE
  I'm sorry I _____ on the trip with you.

6 You can't go to that club if you're under eighteen.
  GOT
  You _____ eighteen to go to that club.

7 It's compulsory to obey the rules if you want to join our gang.
  HAVE
  You _____ the rules if you want to join our gang.

Grammar focus: more modals

5 **Choose the correct answer.**

1 Oh, you *shouldn't have/needn't have* been so unkind to Paula! She was only trying to help.

2 Bob *didn't have to/couldn't have* do detention after all.

3 Conrad *mustn't have/shouldn't have* told a lie, but he did.

4 The gang *might have/must have* left that graffiti on the wall, but I'm not sure.

5 You *ought to have/needed to have* reported the theft to the police.

6 I *needn't have/could have to* texted an apology to Sarah, but I did it anyway.

7 I *could have/might have* killed Jane for posting my secret on Facebook!

8 We knew Sandra was getting the bus here so we *didn't need to get/needn't have got* the car out.

6 **Choose the correct answer, A, B or C.**

1 The burglars _____ broken into the house last night because the alarm was on.
   A needn't have
   B didn't need to
   C couldn't have

2 I _____ worried about starting at my new school because everybody is so friendly.
   A didn't need to
   B couldn't have
   C needn't have

3 You _____ left your keys in the cafeteria. Shall I go back and check?
   A could
   B need have
   C might have

4 You _____ to have left your room in such a mess, Freddie!
   A ought not
   B could not
   C should not

5 Luckily, I had money for a taxi so I _____.
   A needn't have walked
   B couldn't have walked
   C didn't need to walk

6 You shouldn't have cycled on that busy road. You _____ killed!
   A could have been
   B ought to have been
   C might be

7 **Identify the six sentences which contain a mistake and correct them.**

1 Paul can have gone to the party, but I'm not sure.
   Paul could have gone to the party, but I'm not sure.

2 He couldn't be in the café last night. If he were, I'd have seen him.

3 I needn't paid so much for that jacket – I should have gone to another shop.

4 You should have told me you were feeling ill and I would have called a doctor.

5 I'm glad I needn't go to school yesterday – it was great spending time on the beach.

6 Gina isn't here yet – her bus might have broken down.

7 I may leave my phone on the bus so I'd better get back on and look.

8 Tom must have texted Linda, but I'm not sure.

8 **Complete the sentences with one word only.**

1 I think I _may/might_ have hurt Maria's feelings.

2 You ought _____ have discussed the problem with your teacher.

3 It was so nasty of you to say that! You really _____ have apologised for your actions.

4 We didn't _____ to stay late after all because the exam was shorter than we thought.

5 Sally's plane _____ have landed already, but we're not certain.

6 I'm glad I _____ not need to sit next to Carlos today; he's such a bully.

Revision Unit 9

1 Choose the correct word.

1 Clive is really *flexible/generous* – he gives a lot of money away to charity.

2 Somebody who is really *cruel/stubborn* will hurt another person for no reason at all.

3 My brother is so *moody/fussy* that you never know if he's going to be happy or sad from one day to the next.

4 Emma's boyfriend is really *well-mannered/tolerant* – he always holds the door open for women to go first.

5 Using bad language is *unselfish/disrespectful*, especially in front of older people.

6 Teenagers may feel *rebellious/nasty* if they're made to follow too many rules.

7 Mr Lee won't mind if you're late for youth club. He's very *helpful/easy-going*.

8 My little brother is really *disobedient/spiteful* – he never does what my parents tell him to do!

2 Complete the words in the sentences.

1 It was really sp _i_ _t_ _e_ f _u_ l of you to write such cruel remarks about me on Facebook.

2 My gran was w___d_____ when my grandfather was killed in the war.

3 We had a big party to celebrate my sister and her boyfriend getting en_____d. The wedding's next year.

4 Our neighbour only got d_____c___d last year and he's marrying someone new in September!

5 My mum and dad s____p_____d when I was four, so my mum brought me up by herself.

6 I don't just dislike the boy next door; I think he's completely ob_____x_____s.

7 I'm reading a book about a kid who was a_____p_____d by a family of wolves after the death of her parents.

8 One of my brothers accepts what my parents say but the other is a rebel and is always extremely d____f_____t.

3 Choose the correct answer, A, B or C.

1 We only wrote Peter's name on Anne's desk for a _____.
   A smile **B giggle** C grin

2 My teacher hit the _____ when he saw the mess in the classroom.
   A top B ceiling C roof

3 Pamela had a _____ awakening when the exam she'd thought would be easy turned out to be so difficult.
   A shock B cruel C rude

4 Sheila is as hard as _____, so you'll never persuade her to feel sorry for you.
   A nails B metal C iron

5 Ben is a good listener and people often _____ up to him about their problems.
   A give B open C show

6 Babysitting my neighbour's kid was an absolute _____ because he just wouldn't go to sleep.
   A nightmare B dream C torture

4 Complete the text with one word in each space.

Subject: **If you want to be a criminal!**

If you want to be a criminal, you need 1) __to__ have at least a little bit of intelligence. Without it, you 2) _____ try as hard as you like, but you'll end up in prison one day! Take Jason Finch, for example. He decided to rob a bank. He 3) _____ have succeeded, too, if he hadn't written a note for the bank clerk on the back of his own cheque book. When the police arrived they did not 4) _____ to look for fingerprints or clues; they just identified the robber from his cheques and arrested him! One thing you 5) _____ never do as a criminal is to fall asleep on the job. A criminal set out to burgle a house in the USA. He 6) _____ easily have got away with the jewellery but he decided he had 7) _____ lie down on the bed and close his eyes for a few minutes. That bed must 8) _____ been really comfortable because 9) _____ the house owner arrived, the criminal was still fast asleep!

5 Complete the words in the sentences.

1 When criminals come out of jail, a
p _r_ _o_ _b_ at _i_ _o_ n officer often helps them
improve their lives.

2 A criminal is less likely to b_____ g_____ e your
house if you have an alarm fitted.

3 It's not safe to leave your car in this street because
the local gang might v_____ d_____ s____ it.

4 Crazy people sometimes st_____ k celebrities,
which means they follow them round everywhere
they go.

5 People often end up in jail because of their
criminal b____ h____ v_____ .

6 The vandals were too young for jail so they were
put in d_____ e_____ i_____ .

7 The j_____ g_____ told the jury to take as much
time as they wanted to reach a decision.

8 The attacker left his v_____ t_____ m lying in the
street, badly injured.

**6 Rewrite the sentences using the words in
capitals. Use between two and five words,
including the word given.**

1 It's compulsory to follow the rules.
OBEY
You _must/have(got) to_ obey the rules.

2 Their teachers didn't let them leave school early.
ALLOWED
They _____ school early.

3 My advice is to report the bully to the
headteacher.
SHOULD
I think _____ to the headteacher.

4 We were obliged to do chores to earn our
pocket money.
TO
We _____ chores to earn our
pocket money.

5 I worried about the problem but it
wasn't necessary.
NEED
I _____ worried about the problem.

6 It would have been a good idea to text
our parents.
SHOULD
We _____ our parents.

7 It's possible I left my keys in the door.
COULD
I _____ my keys in the door.

**7 Identify the six sentences which contain a mistake
and correct them.**

1 Nobody could prevent the accident yesterday. ✗
Nobody could have prevented the accident yesterday.

2 You should have gone home earlier last night.

3 My parents weren't let to smoke when they
were children.

4 Did you have got to apologise for what you said?

5 I didn't need tell Mike the secret because he
knew already.

6 You must to obey your parents, I'm afraid.

7 Clare may have rung while I was in the shower –
I'll check.

8 When I was younger, I wasn't let to stay up late.

8 Use the clues to solve the crossword.

Across

1 A situation in which neither opponent is winning

2 The person who decides how criminals
are punished

4 An adjective which means hateful

5 If someone breaks the law, a policeman may
_____ them.

7 Jobs around the house

Down

1 Behaviour that shows you refuse to do what
someone tells you to do

3 To admit you are wrong

6 Another word for a quarrel or argument

VOCABULARY

1 Complete the sentences with the correct form of the word in capitals.

1 We saw the famous _portrait_ of King Henry hanging in the National Art Gallery.
PORTRAY

2 There has been great excitement over the _____ of Tutankhamen's tomb.
DISCOVER

3 The castle was destroyed during the great _____ in the 16th century.
REBEL

4 The tyrant was _____ and ordered all his prisoners to be killed.
MERCY

5 The new prince is a _____ of the ancient kings of Scotland.
DESCEND

6 Is there any real _____ that the ruler was murdered?
PROVE

7 I love studying the past and one day I'd like to be a famous _____ .
HISTORY

2 Choose the correct answer.

1 Adolf Hitler was a(n) *unknown/infamous* figure who caused the death of millions of people.

2 Queen Elizabeth I is *unearthed/buried* in Westminster Abbey.

3 Royal families are often buried in beautifully decorated *tombs/trenches*.

4 There are no *records/portraits* of where the last Inca king is buried.

5 I love reading the Greek *rumours/myths*, like the story of Theseus and the Minotaur.

6 In *ancient/aged* times people believed their rulers – the pharaohs – were gods.

7 Archaeologists have discovered the *remains/rests* of a Roman temple.

8 The people who set up the United Nations wanted to prevent a third world *battle/war*.

3 Complete the sentences with these words.

burial   contentious   curse   fever pitch   grave   mankind   mutilated   stumbled upon

1 They put the tyrant's body in an unmarked _grave_ where nobody would find it.

2 The ruler died while sailing round his country, so his _____ took place at sea.

3 Excitement rose to _____ as news of the amazing discovery spread through the country.

4 The king was murdered and parts of his _____ body were put on show round the city.

5 Nobody can agree about the causes of the war; the topic is extremely _____ .

6 Archaeologists _____ the body while they were searching for the remains of a palace.

7 There is a _____ on Tutankhamun's tomb which threatens bad things to anyone who enters it.

8 Throughout the history of _____, there have been many battles and wars.

4 Find ten words on the topic of history. The words go across, down or diagonally. The first letter of each word is highlighted.

a	u	e	z	g	d	g	g	l	e	n	o	a	s	l
r	c	i	r	r	d	f	u	s	d	u	n	n	h	r
e	q	x	o	a	f	r	v	t	m	t	j	e	i	m
u	r	c	o	y	n	r	e	e	r	o	m	i	s	j
k	e	j	y	r	f	e	r	p	x	m	t	j	t	e
r	e	j	f	e	c	m	h	r	x	b	z	b	o	q
r	b	z	q	h	q	a	d	a	m	n	j	x	r	j
e	x	z	a	e	i	i	m	s	a	d	m	w	i	j
b	s	k	v	a	b	n	d	u	q	j	m	k	a	j
e	a	f	f	r	t	s	d	s	t	y	r	a	n	t
l	o	d	e	s	c	e	n	d	a	n	t	q	v	t
l	n	l	o	a	m	w	p	p	m	b	y	e	e	g
i	l	f	g	l	w	g	r	a	v	e	d	d	t	i
o	u	b	n	h	p	k	j	b	u	r	i	a	l	u
n	e	x	c	a	v	a	t	i	o	n	t	n	o	v

5 Match the words and their meanings.

1	downpour	a	An attempt by people in a country to change their government by force
2	upbringing	b	When something bad starts, such as a serious disease or a war
3	outcry	c	The final result of a meeting, process, etc.
4	turnaround	d	The money you receive regularly, e.g. from your work
5	uprising	e	The way your parents care for you and teach you as a child
6	outbreak	f	A complete change from a bad situation to a good one
7	income	g	An angry protest by a lot of people
8	outcome	h	A lot of rain that falls in a short time

6 Make these verbs into nouns ending in the preposition, *down*, *out* or *over*.

1 take + *over* = a *takeover*
2 break + _____ = a _____
3 work + _____ = a _____
4 crack + _____ = a _____
5 hand + _____ = a _____
6 check + _____ = a _____
7 make + _____ = a _____
8 turn + _____ = a _____

7 Complete the sentences by adding a preposition to the verb to make a noun.

1 Have you got a copy of the _handout_ the lecturer gave us? (hand)
2 The police have had a _____ on the numbers of people who drink and drive. (crack)
3 Heavy storms turned the firework party into a complete _____. (wash)
4 There was a _____ on the motorway which caused big traffic jams. (break)
5 I'll wait at the _____ if you run and find the history book you want to buy. (check)
6 The archaeologists were disappointed at the poor _____ for their lecture. (turn)
7 If you're in a bad mood, go to the gym and have a good _____ – it'll make you feel much better! (work)
8 The museum has had a complete _____ and it looks really up to date now! (make)

8 Use the clues to complete the crossword.

Across
3 The parts of something that are left after the other parts have been destroyed
4 Magic words that bring someone bad luck
5 Belonging to a time in history that was thousands of years ago
6 All humans, considered as a group
Down
1 Someone who is related to a person who lived a long time ago
2 When rain stops something from happening, we say it is a _____.

GRAMMAR
Grammar focus: relative clauses

1 Choose the correct word.

1 Is this one of the castles *that/what* you have already visited?

2 Richard is the king *who/whose* nephews were killed in the Tower.

3 Paul's the teacher *who/which* will be teaching us history next term.

4 A dinosaur was an animal *who/which* lived thousands of years ago.

5 She works in a museum *that/it* used to be part of a temple.

6 The town *where/that* I grew up has a long history.

7 Can you remember the date *which/when* the war started?

8 I've just seen the house *where/that* I was born.

2 Complete the sentences by adding the information in brackets. You may need to change the order of the clauses.

1 The Valley of the Kings is a place in Egypt. (The tombs of many Pharaohs were uncovered there.)
   The Valley of the Kings is a place in Egypt where the tombs of many Pharaohs were found.

2 There is a temple in the city.
   (It holds amazing treasures.)

3 The queen's uncle was arrested and executed.
   (He put poison in the king's drink.)

4 Our country has plenty of castles.
   (They are all open to the public most weekdays.)

5 I've just read about a king.
   (His children joined in a rebellion against him.)

6 We took a photo of the palace.
   (The royal family still live in it.)

7 The armour can be seen in the museum.
   (The king fought in it.)

8 The crown is in the museum.
   (I visited it yesterday.)

3 Complete the spaces with appropriate relative or participle clauses using the words in brackets.

1 We visited the tomb, then wrote up our project. (before)
   We visited the tomb *before writing up* our project.

2 We saw the crown jewels, then made our way to the exit. (After)
   ...., we made our way to the exit.

3 When he discovered the buried treasure the boy shouted out loud. (On)
   ...., the boy shouted out loud.

4 Meeting the famous historian was wonderful. (which)
   We met the famous historian, ...

5 I wrote my history essay. I researched it first. (Before)
   ...., I researched it.

6 They broke the lock; they got into the castle. (By)
   .... the lock, they got into the castle.

7 An expert claims to have found an Inca tomb. This has surprised everyone. (which)
   An expert claims to have found the tomb of an Inca king, ...

8 After they had stolen the gold, the pirates sailed away. (Having)
   ...., the pirates sailed away.

4 Find the mistake in each of these sentences and correct it.

1 The palace where the Pharaoh lived it was very beautiful.
   The palace where the pharaoh lived was very beautiful.

2 That was the most interesting museum what I have ever seen.

3 His son, which was next in line to the throne, was murdered.

4 Archaeologists found the body they'd been looking for it.

5 In the book, was written recently, you can read all about the First World War.

6 I loved the castle you took me last year.

Grammar focus: cleft sentences; wh-clauses

5 **Rewrite the sentences starting with the words in brackets.**

1 I'm shocked at how the king behaved.
(What shocks)
What shocks me is how the king behaved.

2 My gran first got me interested in history.
(It was)

3 I'm surprised how long the inhabitants of the castle survived.
(What surprises)

4 During the tour we saw the queen's jewellery.
(What happened)

5 The prisoners were kept in a tiny underground jail.
(The place)

6 I'm interested in how little mankind really changes throughout its history.
(What interests me)

7 I really need some help with my project.
(What I really need)

8 The reason for the princes' deaths was a mystery.
(Why the princes died)

6 **Put the words in the correct order.**

1 with / the historian / didn't / I / said / agree / what
I didn't agree with what the historian said.

2 enjoy / what / you / you / are studying / Do / ?

3 hear / said / what / didn't / you / We / .

4 what / king / remember / did / can't / the / I / .

5 reason / because of / history / The / hate / is / I / the dates / .

6 horrified / tyrant / me / did / What / the / .

7 **Complete the article with one word in each space.**

The Inca civilisation

I've always been interested in the past, but 1) ___it___ was my Spanish teacher who got me interested in American history. The period I enjoy reading about most 2) _____ the time when the Incas ruled Peru. 3) _____ I admire most about their civilisation are the huge monuments and roads they built and the wonderful gold and silver works of art they created. But it is their final great leader, Atahualpa 4) _____ really appeals to my imagination. It was 5) _____ he was the Inca of this great empire that soldiers from Spain, the 'conquistadores' arrived. Their reason for coming to Peru 6) _____, of course, to steal the gold and silver and take it back to Spain. I have never understood 7) _____ Atahualpa agreed to meet the soldiers, but he did. And it was this act of trust 8) _____ led to his death, when the Spanish soldiers broke their promise, killed him, and then attacked and robbed his people. A sad end for a wonderful civilisation.

8 **Rewrite the sentences using the words in capitals. Use between two and five words, including the word given.**

1 My teacher gave me a love of history.
IT
It was my teacher who gave me a love of history.

2 I love exploring the past.
WHAT
_____ exploring the past.

3 She didn't listen to my words.
SAID
She didn't listen to _____.

4 We need more information before we start.
IS
What _____ more information before we start.

5 We love going to museums.
WE
Going to museums _____.

6 Nobody knows the place it happened.
WHERE
_____ is a mystery.

Revision Unit 10

1 Complete the sentences with these words.

> buried   century   ~~death~~   descendant
> outbreak   rehearsal   tyrant   war

1 On the _death_ of Queen Elizabeth, Prince Charles will become king in the UK.

2 John F Kennedy was president of the USA during part of the twentieth _____.

3 At the moment I'm reading about the Second World _____.

4 After they die, do you know where most of the kings and queens of England are _____?

5 Adolf Hitler was a _____ who used his power in such a cruel and unjust way that he caused a war.

6 Prince William is a _____ of Queen Victoria who reigned over the United Kingdom in the nineteenth century.

7 There was a _____ on the day before the royal wedding so the prince and his bride could practise for the big day.

8 Many of the soldiers died due to an _____ of malaria.

2 Choose the best answer, A, B or C.

1 Official _____ of all historic events in our village are kept in the local government office.
  (A) records   **B** memories   **C** remembrances

2 The soldier was buried in a simple, unmarked _____.
  A hole   **B** grave   **C** tomb

3 In 1692, Columbus set out on a long _____ which would take him to America.
  A expedition   **B** exploration   **C** discovery

4 Sending a man to the moon was one of the most fantastic achievements in the history of _____.
  A persons   **B** mankind   **C** people

5 We're studying the history of _____ Greece.
  A ancient   **B** aged   **C** elderly

6 They've just unearthed the _____ of a dinosaur!
  A lasts   **B** rests   **C** remains

3 Complete the sentences with the correct form of the words in capitals.

1 She had a bad _upbringing_ .
  BRING

2 Have they completed the _____ of the Iron Age site?
  EXCAVATE

3 Centuries ago, rulers were often _____ to their victims.
  MERCY

4 We were _____ to hear of the death of the old king.
  SAD

5 The lecture was late starting because of a _____ on the motorway.
  BREAK

6 My friend, Clive claims to be the _____ of a Russian prince!
  DESCEND

7 The Borgias were _____ rulers who robbed and poisoned their people.
  FAMOUS

8 Have you seen the new _____ of Prince William and Kate? It's very lifelike.
  PORTRAY

4 Complete the words in the sentences.

1 The Pharaoh was buried in a magnificent t_o_ _m_ b.

2 The victim's body was so badly m___t_____d that nobody could recognise him.

3 Nobody can agree on the causes of the war – they are very c_____e___t_____us.

4 As the film reached its climax, the audience's excitement grew to f____v____r pitch.

5 Two boys st_____b_____d upon the remains of the dinosaur as they were playing.

6 Claims about the d____s_____y of an Inca grave are being treated with suspicion.

7 Have you got the h_____d_____t the teacher gave us in our last history class?

8 It was a snowy evening, so the t_____n_____t for the lecture was very low.

5 Complete the sentences with one word only.

1 Do you know the date ____when____ war broke out?
2 We saw the castle _____ was destroyed in the rebellion.
3 _____ entering the tomb, the archaeologists found the prince's body.
4 Richard was the king _____ nephews were taken to the Tower.
5 Do you know _____ painted that portrait?
6 What surprises historians _____ that they found the grave so quickly.
7 Dad showed me the place _____ the battle took place.
8 _____ happened to the lost jewels is a mystery.

6 Join the sentences using the relative pronoun in brackets. Use commas only where necessary.

1 The monument is now a tourist site. The Incas built it. (which)
____The monument which the Incas built is now a tourist site.____
2 The king reigned for forty years. His brother tried to kill him. (whose)

3 I know a museum. You can see amazing treasures there. (where)

4 Mr Stone is taking us on the history trip. He's a wonderful teacher. (who)

5 I can't remember the date. John F Kennedy died then. (when)

6 Have you read the news report? It claims they have found an Inca tomb. (which)

7 Complete the article with one word in each space.

8 Rewrite the sentences, using a relative/participle clause.

1 The prince was scared. He rode into battle.
In spite of _being scared_ , the prince rode into battle.
2 Frank didn't realise the object was so ancient. He picked it up in his hands.
Not _____ , Frank picked the object up in his hands.
3 Clare unearthed the gold coins. She shouted in surprise.
After _____ , Clare shouted in surprise.
4 First they finished their research; then they had a coffee.
They finished their research before _____ .
5 Mum had never seen an Egyptian mummy before. She screamed in surprise.
Never _____ , Mum screamed in surprise.
6 We got off the coach. We stared up at the cathedral.
On _____ , we stared up at the cathedral.
7 Emma fell while she was getting off the coach.
While _____ , Emma fell.
8 David didn't speak as he led the way to the castle.
Without _____ , David led the way to the castle.

The **Real** Pirates

These days pirates are often cartoon figures or amusing characters in films like *Pirates of the Caribbean*. But 1) ____what____ we know from history books is that real life pirates were actually very violent. Francois L'Olonnais, 2) _____ was French by nationality, was one of the most infamous. He'd been attacked and nearly killed by Spaniards early on, 3) _____ gave him a lifelong hatred of Spain. He made this clear when, 4) _____ capturing a Spanish ship, he cut off the heads of all its sailors! L'Olonnais did not sail alone. As well as the ship 5) _____ which he travelled, he had seven other ships. He also led hundreds of men, with 6) _____ he terrorised the coast of South America. What he wanted 7) _____ the gold which treasure ships were carrying back to Spain. Many pirates had similar ambitions. However, the 8) _____ why we remember L'Ollonais is because he was merciless; he even ate the heart of a victim to make his friends lead him to hidden treasure. Forget the romance – pirates were some of the cruellest criminals in history!

VOCABULARY

1 Choose the correct word.

1 You shouldn't always give in to peer *pressure/ persuasion.*

2 I've just bought the *last/latest* trainers with my birthday money!

3 I was disappointed with the DVD I bought because it didn't *give/live* up to its promise!

4 If you take your phone back to the shop and explain what's wrong with it they'll give you a *receipt/refund.*

5 The shop assistant had a long line of *customers/ consumers* waiting to pay for their items.

6 If Dan boasts about his trainers to you, just *neglect/ignore* him!

7 Who needs designer *tickets/labels*? I think the people who buy them are just stupid.

8 Kids often *pester/exploit* their parents to buy trendy gadgets.

2 Complete the sentences with these words.

> bargain   buzz   devious   ~~impressionable~~
> pester   status   tempt   trendsetter

1 Advertisers try to influence *impressionable* young people.

2 I love shopping – I get a real _____ out of it!

3 My little sister always tries to _____ my mum into buying her something when we're out.

4 Sam is a real _____ – everyone copies what he wears and does.

5 Some kids want to have the latest gadget as a _____ symbol.

6 Sometimes advertising can be unfair or even completely _____ .

7 The salesperson tried to _____ us to buy something, but we wanted to save our money.

8 Wait until the sales are on in the shops and things are reduced in price – that's when you can find a real _____ .

3 Make adjectives from these words.

1 comfort → *comfortable*
2 patience → _____
3 attract → _____
4 mercy → _____
5 fashion → _____
6 help → _____
7 fortune → _____

4 Complete the sentences with the correct form of the word in capitals.

1 I didn't buy the jeans because they were tight and *uncomfortable* .   COMFORT

2 Ken sighed _____ ; Janet was late again!   PATIENT

3 I don't like the latest fashion trends; in fact some of the styles are really _____ .   ATTRACT

4 Red was the 'in' colour last year, but now it's really _____ .   FASHION

5 Sally wanted to buy trainers like mine, but _____ , they were all sold out.   FORTUNATE

6 I complained about the shop assistant because she was so _____ .   HELP

7 You sometimes get a bit of pain and _____ when you wear shoes for the first time.   COMFORT

8 Mrs France didn't notice her child's _____ until she had paid for her shopping.   APPEAR

5 Find ten words on the topic of fashion and shopping. The words go across, down or diagonally. The first letter of each word is highlighted.

m	n	u	t	t	g	e	n	w	l	a	t	e	s	t
g	v	x	r	n	r	u	j	a	a	l	c	k	p	w
o	s	d	e	b	m	q	e	e	g	c	e	i	j	u
f	k	a	n	u	z	t	j	m	x	s	e	m	m	f
s	k	p	d	z	r	u	o	y	i	c	m	r	h	r
i	o	l	s	z	z	m	h	l	e	r	t	e	a	o
g	x	a	e	u	i	p	a	r	e	l	b	c	b	e
i	d	b	t	q	f	n	k	n	c	c	t	a	t
n	d	e	t	m	o	l	g	h	o	a	e	t	r	g
g	n	l	e	s	r	i	l	b	n	f	t	y	g	m
j	d	q	r	z	s	t	w	o	s	d	t	b	a	q
f	o	e	l	e	i	a	w	r	u	z	u	s	i	h
t	p	v	d	f	g	d	u	q	m	o	t	k	n	k
g	l	i	t	e	r	a	c	y	e	k	l	k	u	u
w	r	e	f	u	n	d	w	v	r	c	b	v	s	d

6 Choose the correct answer.

1 The fashion show was *absolutely/very* good.
2 I've been working *highly/incredibly* hard this morning.
3 That suit looks *very/absolutely* fantastic on you!
4 I was *bitterly/strongly* disappointed at the news.
5 My sister finds walking in such high heels *absolutely/very* impossible.
6 Their latest advertising campaign was *highly/strongly* successful.
7 We found making our own clothes *very/absolutely* difficult, but the end results were great!
8 I'm *utterly/bitterly* convinced I ordered the right size online.

7 Choose the correct answer, A, B, C or D.

1 My dad's _____ to his boss about improving the way they advertise the company.
  A asking   B discussing
  C talking   D interviewing

2 Beth _____ people's awareness of the environmental disaster by posting a clip on YouTube.
  A lifted   B raised
  C helped   D got

3 I had no _____ that advertisers filmed inside teenager's houses.
  A mind   B knowledge
  C though   D idea

4 I've had a lot of work to do recently, but I'm _____ near the end now.
  A going   B getting
  C reaching   D approaching

5 Our parents were _____ concerned about the amount of violence in the TV programme.
  A deeply   B utterly
  C bitterly   D absolutely

6 I haven't seen the advertisement you like, but I'll certainly _____ for it now.
  A look out   B put up
  C make up   D go in

7 I _____ ban advertisements on television if I had the choice!
  A could   B need
  C would   D ought

8 When my friend told me I could be a model, I never gave it a second _____.
  A mind   B thought
  C idea   D opinion

8 Complete the words in the sentences.

1 Something that's the most recent or the newest is called the l *a* t *e* *s* t.
2 If you are d___v_____ us, you use tricks or lies to get what you want.
3 Someone who is imp_____ion_____ is easy to influence.
4 A tr_____d is the latest fashion style.
5 If you t_____t someone, you make them want to do something.
6 If you p_____r someone, you ask them to do something many times.
7 Something you own that suggests you are rich or powerful is a s_____s symbol.
8 Someone who buys or uses goods or services is a c_____s___m___r.

GRAMMAR
Grammar focus: wishes and regrets

1 **Choose the correct answer.**

1 I wish you *came/could come* to the party!
2 Sophie wishes she *wouldn't have bought/hadn't bought* that ring.
3 I wish you *were/would be* coming on holiday with us.
4 If only I *had/would have* more pocket money!
5 Glen regrets *to get/getting* that tattoo now.
6 I wish the sun *came out/would come out*, but it's still cloudy.
7 We wish we *didn't eat/hadn't eaten* so much last night.
8 I wish they *stopped/would stop* putting so many ads on TV.

2 **Complete the sentences with these verbs and any other necessary words.**

> drive   give   have to   let   spend   stop   tell   warn

1 She regrets _*telling*_ Paul her secret.
2 I haven't got any pocket money left. I wish I _____ it all!
3 James wishes he _____ his dad's car, but he's not allowed to.
4 Ella regrets _____ her phone number to Alan.
5 If only I _____ to attend school every day! I'd much rather stay at home.
6 Do you regret _____ Simon use your phone?
7 If only the teacher _____ us that we were having a test!
8 I can't get to sleep because my brother's in the next bed. If only he _____ snoring!

3 **Complete the sentences using the words in brackets in the correct form.**

1 I wish you _would listen_ (listen) to me! You haven't heard a word I've said!
2 I wish I _____ (not/have to) leave now!
3 Gemma regrets _____ (promise) to meet Peter tonight.
4 I really miss you. I wish you _____ (sit) near me now!
5 Don't you wish you _____ (be) a bit older?
6 I wish I _____ (drive), but I'm too young.

4 **Rewrite the sentences, using the word in capitals.**

1 Mum is sad because she can't take a day off work.
SHE
Mum wishes _she could take_ a day off work.
2 I'm sorry I bought this album now.
WISH
I _____ that album now.
3 Beth wishes she hadn't swapped her jacket.
SWAPPING
Beth _____ her jacket.
4 What a pity you didn't text me!
ONLY
If _____ me!
5 I'm sad you're not here.
YOU
I _____ here!
6 George is sorry he shouted at you.
REGRETS
George _____ at you.
7 I'm sad I'm not going shopping with you.
GO
I wish I _____ with you.
8 Amy is sad she's not sitting on a beach now.
WISHES
Amy _____ on a beach now.

Grammar focus: it's time, would rather

5 Choose the correct answer.

1 It's time Alfie *cleaned/would clean* his shoes!

2 We'd rather *not to watch/not watch* that film tonight.

3 Hurry up! It's time *to go/we go*!

4 I *would/had* rather you didn't speak to me like that!

5 Isn't it time you *went/go* home?

6 Wendy would rather we *give/gave* her money for her birthday.

7 It's time you *got/would get* your hair cut!

8 I'd rather *play/playing* computer games than go shopping.

6 Complete the sentences with one word only.

1 I'd rather you ____were____ my friend than my enemy!

2 I'd _____ Carla didn't borrow my things all the time.

3 I think it's _____ we went to bed.

4 It's time to _____ the TV off now.

5 I _____ rather have love than money!

6 Hurry up! It's time _____ leave.

7 I know you'd like to kiss me, but I'd rather _____ didn't!

8 We'd _____ leave the barbecue until next week, if that's OK?

7 Find the mistake in each of these sentences and correct it.

1 1'd rather you don't call me that!
   I'd rather you didn't call me that!

2 It's time Oscar goes home now!
   _____

3 I had rather you did not go out tonight.
   _____

4 We'd rather to walk than to drive.
   _____

5 Do you think it's time we take the cake out of the oven?
   _____

6 It's time I stop texting and do some homework, I'm afraid.
   _____

8 Complete the blog with one word in each space.

Advertisers are targeting teenagers   ⇦ ⇨

💬 View previous comments   Cancel   Share   Post

Advertisers are targeting teenagers more and more. So I think 1) ____it____ is high time we protested about the tricks they use to make us buy things. They want us 2) _____ believe that buying a product will make us look trendier or more attractive. They 3) _____ rather we worried about how we look to our friends than considered whether we need a product or not. They'd also 4) _____ play on our fears of being left out than make us feel good. It's time 5) _____ fight back! Next time you see an advert online or on TV, ask 6) _____ some questions. Isn't it 7) _____ advertisers stopped interrupting our activities to exploit us in this way? Is it fair to use things like product placement and peer pressure so often 8) _____ we don't even realise how much we're being influenced. What do *you* think?

Write a comment   Support

Revision Unit 11

1 Choose the correct answer, A, B, C or D.

1 We were _____ disappointed with the laptops we bought.
2 These trainers were a half-price _____ in the sales!
3 Advertisers think all teenagers want to wear designer _____.
4 Keep your _____ in case you want to return the jacket to the shop.
5 I felt _____ to buy a new sports bag but my friend stopped me.
6 That jacket looks _____ good on you!
7 My shoes are the _____ fashion – do you like them?
8 My dad's boss drives a Mercedes; it's a status _____.

1	(A) bitterly	B	strongly	C	highly	D	absolutely
2	A cost	B	product	C	buzz	D	bargain
3	A posters	B	labels	C	tablets	D	marks
4	A refund	B	note	C	receipt	D	paper
5	A nagged	B	tempted	C	pestered	D	attracted
6	A absolutely	B	very	C	highly	D	strongly
7	A last	B	late	C	latest	D	newest
8	A style	B	trend	C	look	D	symbol

2 Complete the sentences with the correct form of the word in capitals.

1 I'll have to stand up – this chair is really _uncomfortable_.
   COMFORT
2 Teenagers are often quite _____ young people.
   IMPRESS
3 Gemma's boyfriend is very _____; how did she find someone so good-looking?
   ATTRACT
4 Mum's in hospital and she's in some _____ with her broken leg.
   COMFORT
5 I'd like a pizza, but I haven't got any money, _____.
   FORTUNE
6 Ken is stylish, but his brother's clothes are so _____!
   FASHION
7 I'm coming! Don't be so _____!
   PATIENCE
8 I asked a man the way to the shop, but he was really _____.

   HELP

3 Choose the correct word.

1 The _critically_/bitterly acclaimed film won an Oscar.
2 I'm _utterly_/incredibly convinced that there should be strict rules about advertising to children.
3 The time is passing incredibly/_highly_ slowly this morning!
4 Advertisers have been deeply/_highly_ successful at targeting teens.
5 My dad bitterly/_highly_ objects to paying such high prices for petrol.
6 What you just told me is strongly/_absolutely_ absurd!
7 The advertising campaign was strongly/_highly_ successful.
8 These days the cost of living is utterly/_ridiculously_ high.

4 Complete the definitions. The first and last letters are given.

1 An adjective to describe someone who uses tricks or lies to get what they want is
   d _e v i o u_ s.
2 A verb that means _to make someone want to do something_ is t_____t.
3 Someone who buys or uses goods or services is a c_____r.
4 The latest fashion style is called a t_____d.
5 A verb that means to _decorate something in your own way to show it belongs to you_ is
   p_____e.
6 The money you're given back in a shop if what you've bought is not satisfactory is a r_____d.
7 Someone who is a leader of fashion is a t_____r.
8 The piece of paper that shows you have paid for something is a r_____t.

5 **Find the mistakes in the sentences and correct them.**

1 It's time we go.
   It's time we went.

2 I wish you are here!
   _____

3 She regrets to taking the sweets without paying for them.
   _____

4 I'd rather not to see that film.
   _____

5 I wish you didn't play that music – it's awful!
   _____

6 It's time we leave for the party!
   _____

7 Oh no, I'm late! If only the bus came.
   _____

8 I'd rather Paul he didn't come with us.
   _____

6 **Complete the sentences with one word.**

1 I wish you _____were_____ here.
2 If only we _____ afford a holiday!
3 I think it's _____ we went to bed.
4 I really _____ arguing with Stella; it was stupid of me.
5 Hurry up! It's time _____ leave!
6 I'd rather _____ didn't tell Mum where I was last night!
7 I wish I _____ brought my umbrella.
8 Do you regret _____ so much money for that watch?

7 **Complete the article with one word in each space.**

8 **Use the clues to complete the crossword.**

Across

2 If something lives up to its _____ , it is as good as people said it would be.
4 When you look at things in shops without intending to buy them
5 A strong feeling that you must do the same things as other people of your age if you want them to like you.
6 A feeling of excitement
7 To make someone do something by explaining why it is a good idea

Down

1 Clothes made by a famous fashion designer
3 To annoy someone by asking them to do something many times

Teen opinion This Week: Advertising!

For our teen opinion page this week, we thought it 1) _____was_____ time we conducted a teen survey on advertising. Here's a summary of your ideas. It seems most of you enjoy watching adverts if they're funny and well-made but you wish advertisers would 2) _____ people choose when to watch them. '3) _____ only they'd stop interrupting our favourite TV shows!' was a typical comment in the survey.

It seems you don't trust brands either, so in future advertisers may regret 4) _____ so much money putting recognisable designs on their products. It seems you'd 5) _____ not be left behind if your friends have certain products, but the picture is confusing here. 'Sometimes I wish I 6) _____ stand out more and be different, but other times I just want 7) _____ fit in' was a typical comment here. Most of you have no income except pocket money, and you wish advertisers 8) _____ remember that and realise you are looking for products that are good value and reflect your personality.

VOCABULARY

1 **Label the activities in the pictures.**

A

B

....

C

D

....

E

F

....

2 **Choose the correct answer, A, B or C.**

1 Some extreme sports involve putting your life
.... risk.
A in **B** over **C** at

2 White-water rafting gave me a real
adrenaline ....
A hurry **B** speed **C** rush

3 For our geography trip, we're going on an
overland ....!
A voyage **B** expedition **C** travel

4 Crossing the desert in such hot temperatures
was a real ....
A challenge **B** attempt **C** contest

5 Our hotel was off the beaten ....
A way **B** track **C** road

6 I'm glad my parents don't try to .... me in
cotton wool.
A capture **B** tie **C** wrap

7 I'd like to be a wildlife presenter and follow in
David Attenborough's ....
A footsteps **B** footmarks **C** footprints

8 I'd like a holiday in a really exotic ....
A station **B** destination **C** stop

3 **Complete the sentences with the correct preposition.**

1 Going ....*on*........ an expedition must be
great fun.

2 My parents frowned .... the idea of
us going on holiday alone.

3 We took part .... all the activities.

4 I had to run to keep .... with
my friends.

5 I'd like to try my hand .... skiing.

6 Ralph wasn't allowed to go ....
the trip.

7 Our campsite was .... the
beaten track.

4 Complete the words in the sentences.

1 You wear g _o_ _g_ _g_ _l_ _e_ s to protect your eyes when you're diving.
2 We stopped to admire the qu _____ t, little houses in the village.
3 My parents made me look at lots of an _____ nt monuments.
4 Spain is my favourite holiday des _____ a _____ on.
5 My sister wants to go on a solo v _____ e round the world in her own boat.
6 I like holidays that set you some kind of ch _____ ll _____ .

5 Choose the correct word.

1 Zac broke the world *challenge/record.*
2 The village was very pretty and had lots of *white-washed/sandy* cottages.
3 We saw plenty of *aged/ancient* monuments.
4 The hotel was on a long, *bending/winding* road.
5 Our summer holiday was packed with *non-stop/up-down* excitement.
6 The people were very *hospitable/scenic.*
7 We saw photos of *quaint/sun-kissed* beaches.
8 Let me see those *break/holiday* brochures!

6 Find ten words on the topic of holidays and adventure. The words go across, down or diagonally. The first letter of each word is highlighted.

u	t	r	e	k	k	i	n	g	e	u	t	u	f	z
v	w	p	z	h	t	e	k	h	m	a	l	o	b	y
k	t	m	x	s	w	c	q	t	p	y	p	n	s	n
f	n	b	r	v	i	e	w	s	y	a	g	c	x	p
n	b	n	i	r	f	t	m	r	n	i	p	n	p	z
n	l	m	s	n	s	c	u	w	z	v	o	k	c	j
x	f	w	k	g	z	u	z	j	e	i	z	z	h	t
t	b	m	o	z	l	w	m	q	t	g	e	e	a	c
p	a	r	a	g	l	i	d	i	n	g	g	z	l	v
s	h	b	r	x	s	b	d	i	a	g	o	j	l	k
c	b	r	r	i	t	e	p	y	t	f	x	h	e	l
e	s	b	m	e	p	m	o	q	c	e	s	y	n	i
n	n	t	g	x	a	v	c	o	p	p	b	s	g	w
i	p	v	e	c	r	k	f	f	p	u	k	y	e	o
c	w	h	a	s	b	o	c	r	w	o	m	y	n	b

7 Complete the sentences with compound adjectives, using the words in brackets.

1 I write with my right hand, but I see you are *left-handed* . (left/hand)
2 Diane gave an _____ scream as the hang glider rose higher. (ear/split)
3 My skiing instructor is _____ . (kind/heart)
4 I'm hungry and that pizza looks absolutely _____ ! (mouth/water)
5 If something goes wrong in an extreme sport, it can have _____ consequences. (far-reach)
6 I like people who don't criticise everything and are _____ . (open/mind)

8 Complete the article with the correct form of the word in brackets.

View previous comments   Cancel   Share   Post

Extreme danger!
Would you take part in an extreme sport if you were given the 1) _choice_ (choose)? I'd always wanted to try caving even though it sounded quite a 2) _____ (scare) thing to do. So when my friend Steve suggested we have a go, I said 'yes'. I didn't tell my parents because I knew what their 3) _____ (react) would be. 'It's too dangerous. You can't go', they'd warn me. So, although I felt 4) _____ (guilt) about it, I said nothing. Everything went well as we climbed down into the cave. It was a bit 5) _____ (smell) but the rock formations were really 6) _____ (impress)! And it was so 7) _____ (peace) down there! We went further and further underground and the hole we were in got narrower and narrower. Then we had a 8) _____ (dread) shock. The hole was too small for us to go on – and there was no room to turn round and go back. We were stuck in the cave!

Write a comment   Support

GRAMMAR
Grammar focus: modal verbs for degrees of certainty

1 **Choose the correct answer, A, B or C.**

1 The house is empty, so Mum _____ out.
  A must go
  B must have gone *(circled)*
  C must be going

2 Your dad _____ very happy when you broke your surfboard.
  A can't be
  B can't feel
  C can't have been

3 Tom's hands _____ when he dived from such a high rock.
  A must have been shaking
  B can have been shaking
  C can have shaken

4 Rock climbing is hard, so it's possible you _____ some training.
  A can need
  B may need
  C must need

5 Clare _____ sailing or she wouldn't spend so much time on it.
  A can be loving
  B must have loved
  C must love

6 Alfie gave up kite-surfing a long time ago, so he _____ it much.
  A can't have enjoyed
  B mustn't be enjoying
  C may not be enjoying

7 Sam _____ the race, but I'm not sure.
  A must have won
  B might have won
  C can have won

8 Our safari guide _____ very carefully or he would have seen the tiger first!
  A can't look
  B can't be looking
  C can't have been looking

2 **Complete the sentences using the prompts.**

1 Our neighbours have won a free holiday! They / must / run round their house and cheering!
  They must be running round their house and cheering!

2 I'm worried Ella's not here yet. She / might / get lost!

3 Gran brought up my dad by herself. That can't / be easy.

4 Get off the telephone, Jack! All the time you're using it, someone / might / try / to telephone me.

5 My mobile's not in my pocket! Someone / must / steal it.

6 Look how many old postcards Finn has. He / must / collect /them for ages!

7 Robert hasn't come out of school yet; he may / get detention.

8 That car's crashed into the bus in front; the driver / can't / pay attention.

3 **Look at the pictures and complete the sentences using the verb in brackets.**

1 He _must know_ (must/know) the answer.
2 Our neighbours _____ (must/go) on holiday.
3 She _____ (can/not/look) where she was going.
4 Someone _____ (might/tell him off).
5 He _____ (can/not/win) the lottery.
6 Emma _____ (must/break) her leg!

4 **Find the mistakes in the parts of the sentences in italics and correct them.**

1 Mum isn't here – she *might to be* next door.
2 George has left all his dinner, *so he can't be liking it.*
3 Look at the clouds – *I think it can rain soon.*
4 *Laura can't leave for the airport yet* because her suitcase is still here.
5 William's face was very red, *so he must felt embarrassed.*
6 Maria ignored John at the party, so *she can't be liking him very much.*
7 You didn't look hot, so you *couldn't be cycling very fast.*
8 My phone isn't working; *the battery might it be flat.*

5 Rewrite the sentences using the words in capitals. Use between two and five words, including the word given.

1 It's not likely they had a good holiday because they look so depressed.
ENJOYED
They _can't have enjoyed_ a good holiday because they look so depressed.

2 I'm not sure if Sally is going to Africa.
MIGHT
Sally _____ to Africa, but I'm not sure.

3 There's no postcard here from Mike, so my guess is he forgot to send one.
MUST
There's no postcard here from Mike, so he _____ to send one.

4 I think it's impossible that the ship was travelling so fast.
HAVE
The ship _____ so fast.

5 It's possible we'll go on safari, but it's not certain.
MAY
We _____, but it's not certain.

6 It's not possible the plane has left yet.
CAN'T
The plane _____ yet.

7 I don't believe you're serious!
BE
You _____ joking!

Grammar focus: indefinite pronouns

6 Choose the correct answer.

1 I'm not going *nowhere/anywhere* for my holidays.
2 There's *someone/something* really scary about that castle!
3 My dad's been nearly *anywhere/everywhere* in America.
4 There was *anything/nothing* good about my last holiday!
5 Our usual hotel was booked up, so now we haven't got *anywhere/somewhere* to stay.
6 *Someone/Anyone* should tell those people to be less noisy!
7 I've looked *somewhere/everywhere* for my sunglasses, but I can't find them!
8 I went to the campsite to find you, but no one *was/wasn't* there.

7 Complete the text with one word in each space.

The Trouble with Oscar

I'm going on holiday with my crazy friend, Oscar next year. My parents say I 1) _must be_ be mad. Why? Because 2) _____ Oscar and I are together, 3) _____ goes wrong. I'll give you an example. Last week, Oscar and I had 4) _____ to do, so we decided to hang out in the park. 5) _____ we looked, we could see guys doing fun things, like practising extreme bike tricks. Oscar has always wanted to try this, so he asked a boy, James, to lend him his bike. James can't 6) _____ been thinking straight, because he agreed! Everything was OK until Oscar got ambitious. He tried to jump onto a wall, missed — and he and the bike hit 7) _____ ground hard! Oscar was OK — but the bike wasn't. Luckily, one of the other guys came to help. I didn't get his name but 8) _____ he was, he was brilliant! He got out some tools and repaired the bike then and there. James will never speak to us again, though! So Oscar, you see, is trouble!

8 Complete the sentences with *whoever*, *whatever*, *whenever*, or *wherever*.

1 I hope my friend Sam's having a good holiday, _wherever_ she is.
2 _____ shares a room with my brother will discover that he talks in his sleep.
3 Dad says I have to text him when our plane lands, _____ the time.
4 _____ I go camping, it always rains!
5 I can take _____ I like on our next trip, so I'm going to choose Carla.
6 _____ I go, my little sister follows me!
7 Are you tired? We can go back to the campsite _____ you like.
8 Don't forget to pack the sun cream, _____ you do!

Revision Unit 12

1 **Choose the correct answer, A, B, C or D.**

1 Your success in the sailing competition was really _____ .
   - **A** attractive   **(B)** impressive
   - **C** interesting   **D** sensitive

2 Dad would never have booked such a terrible hotel if he'd been thinking _____ .
   - **A** straight   **B** well
   - **C** right   **D** good

3 I tried to persuade my brother to lend me his new tent, but he was having _____ of it.
   - **A** nothing   **B** anything
   - **C** none   **D** something

4 I'd really love to try my _____ at kite surfing.
   - **A** arm   **B** foot
   - **C** head   **D** hand

5 Don't walk so quickly! I can't keep _____ with you!
   - **A** on   **B** off
   - **C** up   **D** in

6 Trekking through the jungle in that heat was a terrible _____ .
   - **A** ordeal   **B** torture
   - **C** deal   **D** work

7 Our teacher _____ on the idea of sleeping under the stars; she insisted we slept in tents.
   - **A** refused   **B** frowned
   - **C** complained   **D** banned

8 His _____ to sail solo round the world ended in disaster.
   - **A** effort   **B** trial
   - **C** go   **D** attempt

2 **Match an activity with a definition.**

1 rowing

2 abseiling

3 canoeing

4 caving

5 diving

6 paragliding

7 surfboarding

a Standing on a plastic board so that you can ride the ocean waves

b Flying/gliding slowly through the air attached to a parachute shaped like a wing

c Going down a large, natural hole in the side of a hill, or under the ground

d Jumping into water with your head and arms first

e Making a small boat move across the water using long sticks called oars

f Paddling along in a long, narrow boat which is pointed at both ends

g Sliding down a rope and pushing against the wall or cliff with your feet

3 **Complete the sentences with the correct form of the word in capitals.**

1 I found hang-gliding a really _____scary_____ experience.   SCARE

2 The village we stayed in was a bit too _____ for me!   PEACE

3 Walking in the jungle made me all hot and _____ .   SWEAT

4 The panoramic views from the top of the castle were extremely _____ .   IMPRESS

5 After a while, we had to let some air into the tent because it was so _____ .   STUFF

6 We complained because the air conditioning in our hotel room was _____ .   FAULT

7 The walls of our hostel were painted with lovely, _____ designs.   COLOUR

8 Your _____ of holiday sounds great!   CHOOSE

4 **Complete the sentences with compound adjectives formed from the words in brackets.**

1 My friends all write with their right hands but I'm _left-handed_ . (left/hand)

2 Marco comes from the south of Italy so he's quite _____ . (dark/skin)

3 I wish my dad wasn't so _____ . (short/temper)

4 If people are _____ (open/mind), they are willing to consider new ideas and opinions.

5 My grandad is so _____ (kind/heart) – he'd do anything for anyone!

6 I used to think sharks were _____ (cold/blood) killers, but I don't any more.

7 Pamela's decision to give up university had _____ (far/reach) consequences.

8 Our tour guide was tall, _____ (long/hair) and suntanned.

5 **Find the mistakes in the sentences and correct them.**

1   Oh no! I must leave my aeroplane ticket in the car!
    Oh no! I must have left my aeroplane ticket in the car!

2   I went to Paula's house, but nobody wasn't there.

3   Brian must not be staying all week – I'm not sure.

4   I've got anything to wear to the disco tonight.

5   It's only six o'clock. She mustn't have gone to bed yet!

6   Listen, anybody! I want you all to come to our party tonight.

7   I can't believe a word he's saying. He must tell lies!

8   She's been nearly anywhere in Europe except the United Kingdom.

6 **Rewrite the sentences using the word in capitals. Use between two and five words, including the word given.**

1   I was scared by the film.
    REALLY
    The film was *really scary*.

2   It's impossible that you booked the room because there's no record of it.
    HAVE
    You _____ booked the room because there's no record of it.

3   The house was empty when I called.
    WAS
    _____ at home when I called.

4   The room smelled extremely bad.
    VERY
    The room was _____ .

5   It's possible Gary is trying to phone you right now.
    MIGHT
    Gary _____ phone you right now.

6   I'm sure we're too late for the plane.
    MISSED
    We _____ the plane.

7   There's no noise outside.
    VERY
    It is _____ outside.

7 **Complete the sentences with a word beginning with *some-*, *any-*, *every-*, or *no-*.**

1   Has ___*anyone*___ seen Amanda? I think she's lost.

2   _____ has left their handbag on the coach!

3   We had no complaints about our holiday; _____ enjoyed it.

4   I phoned the holiday company, but there was _____ there to answer the phone.

5   Is there _____ at all I can do to help?

6   We've got to find _____ to stay overnight.

7   If you've missed the only flight, there's _____ anyone can do about it.

8   I've looked for my passport, but I can't find it _____ .

8 **Use the clues to complete the crossword.**

Across

1   An adjective used to describe a place or road which has beautiful views of the countryside

4   An adjective to describe food that looks and tastes really good

7   An adjective meaning *friendly and welcoming to visitors*

8   An adjective meaning *curving or bending many times*, usually used to describe a road or path

Down

2   An adjective which means *without stopping*

3   Something you probably don't want your parents to wrap you in

5   An adjective which is used to describe houses whose walls are painted white

6   An adjective which is used to describe a very loud, high scream

Exam information

The *Cambridge English: First for Schools* is made up of four papers, each testing a different area of ability in English. The Reading and Use of English Paper is worth 40 percent of the marks (80 marks), and each of the other papers is worth 20 percent (40 marks each). There are five grades. A, B and C are pass grades; D and E are fail grades.

Reading and Use of English (1 hour 15 minutes)

Part 1 Multiple-choice cloze	*Focus*	Vocabulary/Lexico grammatical
	Task	You read a text with eight gaps. You choose the best word or phrase to fit in each gap from a set of four options (A, B, C or D).
Part 2 Open cloze	*Focus*	Grammar/Lexico grammatical
	Task	You read a text with eight gaps. You have to think of the best word to fill each gap. No options are provided.
Part 3 Word formation	*Focus*	Vocabulary/Lexico grammatical
	Task	You read a text with eight gaps. You are given the stems of the missing words. You have to change each word to fit the context.
Part 4 Key word transformations	*Focus*	Grammar and vocabulary
	Task	There are six items. You are given a sentence and a 'key word'. You have to complete a second, gapped sentence using the key word. The second sentence has a different grammatical structure but must have a similar meaning to the original.
Part 5 Multiple-choice questions	*Focus*	Detail, opinion, attitude, text organisation features, tone, purpose, main idea, implication, meaning from context.
	Task	There are six four-option multiple-choice questions. You have to choose the correct option (A, B, C or D) based on the information in the text.
Part 6 Gapped text	*Focus*	Understanding text structure, cohesion, coherence
	Task	You read a text from which six sentences have been removed and placed in jumbled order after the text. There is one extra sentence that you do not need to use. You must decide from where in the text the sentences have been removed.
Part 7 Multiple matching	*Focus*	Specific information, detail, opinion and attitude
	Task	You read ten questions or statements and a text which has been divided into sections, or several short texts. You have to decide which section or text contains the information relating to each question or statement.

Writing (1 hour 20 minutes)

		The Writing paper has two parts, and you have to complete one task from each part.
Part 1	*Focus*	Outlining and discussing issues and opinions on a particular topic
	Task	Part 1 is compulsory, and there is no choice of questions. You have to write an essay based on a title and notes. You have to write 140–190 words.
Part 2	*Focus*	Writing a task for a particular purpose based on a specific topic, context and target reader.
	Task	Part 2 has four tasks to choose from which may include: • a letter or email • an article • a report • a review • an essay • a story. The fourth option is based on a set text. You have to write 140–190 words for Part 2.

Listening (approximately 40 minutes)

Part 1 **Extracts with multiple-choice questions**	*Focus*	Each extract will have a different focus, which could be: main point, detail, purpose or location of speech, relationship between the speakers, attitude or opinion of the speakers.
	Task	You hear eight short, unrelated extracts of about thirty seconds each. They may be monologues or conversations. You have to answer one three-option multiple-choice question (A, B or C) for each extract.
Part 2 **Sentence completion**	*Focus*	Specific information, detail, stated opinion
	Task	You hear a monologue or conversation lasting about three minutes. You complete ten sentences with words from the text.
Part 3 **Multiple matching**	*Focus*	Gist, detail, function, attitude, purpose, opinion
	Task	You hear a series of five monologues or exchanges, lasting about thirty seconds each. The speakers in each extract are different, but the situations or topics are all related to each other. You have to match each speaker to one of six statements or questions (A–F). There is one extra option that you do not need to use.
Part 4 **Multiple-choice questions**	*Focus*	Specific information, opinion, attitude, gist, main idea
	Task	You hear an interview or conversation which lasts about three minutes. There are seven questions. You have to choose the correct option (A, B or C).

Speaking (approximately 14 minutes)

You take the Speaking test with a partner. There are two examiners. One is the 'interlocutor', who speaks to you, and the other is the 'assessor', who just listens.

Part 1 **Interview** (3 minutes)	*Focus*	General interactional and social language
	Task	The interlocutor asks each of you questions about yourself, such as where you come from, what you do in your free time.
Part 2 **Individual long turn** (4 minutes)	*Focus*	Organising your ideas, comparing, describing, expressing opinions
	Task	The interlocutor gives you two photographs to compare, and to give a personal reaction to. You speak by yourself for about a minute while your partner listens. Then the interlocutor asks your partner a question related to the topic. Only a short answer is expected. You then change roles.
Part 3 **Collaborative task** (3 minutes)	*Focus*	Interacting with your partner, exchanging ideas, expressing and justifying opinions, agreeing and/or disagreeing, suggesting, speculating, evaluating, reaching a decision through negotiation
	Task	You are given a task to discuss together, based on a set of pictures. You should try to reach a conclusion together, but there is no right or wrong answer to the task, and you don't have to agree with each other. It is the interaction between you that is important.
Part 4 **Discussion** (4 minutes)	*Focus*	Expressing and justifying opinions, agreeing and disagreeing
	Task	The interlocutor asks you both general questions related to the topic of Part 3, and gives you the chance to give your opinions on other aspects of the same topic.

Pearson Education Limited
Edinburgh Gate
Harlow
Essex CM20 2JE
England
and Associated Companies throughout the world.

www.pearsonelt.com

First published 2014
Fifth impression 2017

ISBN: 978-1-4479-1395-5

Set in 10pt Mixage ITC Std
Printed in Malaysia (CTP-PJB)

Acknowledgements
*The publishers and author would like to thank the following people for
their feedback and comments during the development of the material:*

Elif Berk, Turkey; Alan Del Castillo Castellanos, Mexico; Dilek Kokler,
Turkey; Trevor Lewis, The Netherlands; Nancy Ramirez, Mexico;
Jacqueline Van Mil-Walker, The Netherlands

The publisher would like to thank the following for their kind
permission to reproduce their photographs:

(Key: b-bottom; c-centre; l-left; r-right; t-top)

Alamy Images: Andy Harmer 55br, Kumar Sriskandan 39c, sdbphoto.
com 23bl; **Corbis:** Dean Pictures 32cr, Hello Lovely 47br, Howard Pyle
/ The Gallery Collection 63br, Image Source 9br, Matthias Kulka 19tr,
Ocean 12br, 43tr, 43cr, Ocean 12br, 43tr, 43cr, Ocean 12br, 43tr, 43cr,
Sigrid Olsson / PhotoAlto 5bl; **Creatas:** 10cr; **Digital Vision:** 10tr;
DK Images: Andy Crawford 20bl, Sarah Ashun 46tl, Suzanne Porter /
Rough Guides 61cr; **Fotolia.com:** antiksu 20br, audrey liverneaux 10bl,
Gina Sanders 20tl, Gokychan 10cl, hotshotsworldwide 10br, Irmina
Mamot 70cr, Jakub Cejpek 70cl, Javier Cuadrado 13cr, Lida Salatian
70bl, mgkuijpers 10tc, Nikolai Sorokin 20cr, Richard Carey 10tl,
Rocco D'Auria 70br, Tyler Olson 43tl, WavebreakmediaMicro 27br;
Getty Images: Jim Dyson 35bl, luismmolina 46c, Mark S Cosslett
71br, svetikd 64br, Thomas Grass 31c, World Perspectives 17cr; **Rex
Features:** 28cr, Cultura 73cr, Jenny Goodall / Daily Mail 15bc, Mantyla
48br, Quirky China News 7tr, Universal History Archive / Universal
Images Group 58tc; **Shutterstock.com:** CandyBox Images 70tr,
EpicStockMedia 70tl, gorillaimages 43cl, Pixsooz 69br, Steve Davis
52cr, StockThings 59tl; **Sozaijiten:** 20tr, 20cl, 20tr, 20cl; **Studio 8:** 45tr;
SuperStock: 37br, Radius 24cr, Science Photo Library 21br, Voisin /
Phanie 51br

Cover images: *Front:* **Shutterstock.com:** Alexander Yakovlev

All other images © Pearson Education

Every effort has been made to trace the copyright holders and we
apologise in advance for any unintentional omissions. We would be
pleased to insert the appropriate acknowledgement in any subsequent
edition of this publication.